Re-poh
Thresholds

By Katie L. Ohlheiser, MSW
(Yurok, Karuk, Redwood Creek)

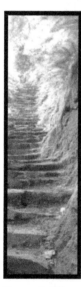

ISBN-13: 978-1466303058 ISBN-10: 1466303050

This contemporary book was written from the perspective of only one modern day Native American woman, often taking a commonplace viewpoint, and using words and phrases of *common knowledge.* The work is not intended to exploit or glorify any person, culture or ethnicity. There is no special effort made to explain the details of culture, but rather to speak from this perspective. It is an introduction to cultural competence by attempting to bridge understandings between *professional* and *minority* populations. There is no intention to be all inclusive. These are writings on many facets of being human.

The pages were often written in the first person tense to invite the reader to consider examining how he or she operates in the world and to *own* the message. The writings, recipes and poems are created from true stories and perspectives including the personal life of the author. As Human Beings share life experiences in common, any similarity to any one person living or dead is merely coincidental except where permissions have been granted.

The hope is to provide insight into the value of diversity and other ways of being in the world within the limitations of the vocabulary available. Poetics can be a running stream of consciousness or take a position, but there are no absolutes. The words are only a *mark in time* as language and time are both malleable. The speech may sound the same as English, but there are purposeful nuances demonstrating worldview where One may perceive a *typo.* The reader is invited to consider that sometimes the answers sought are received when One comes full circle and understands the entire story (including the story behind the story, what is not seen and any contradictions).

Creator, Earth, Great Spirit, two-mo-lek' hoo-le-nee-chok'
kaa-mee-hlek' weehl-kwok' wey-pe-geyrte-lo-gehl
ke'-yo-ne-mek' 'oh-chek' a'h-te-meyr hlkyor-kwee-shon
ho-geee-sek' no-so-no-wok' we-ga'-sok-see-mek'
me-gee'-re-pek' so-ne-nee
wok-hlew wok-hlew wok-hlew

[9]

DEDICATION:

To all my relatives before me, and all my relatives after me; To my friends and those who never gave up on me, my muses, my nemeses, my loves, my amazing teachers, the people who took me in and showed me kindness; To the people who will read this and realize that there is a different way of thinking that can be just as valid as what is familiar; To the last of the Great Redwoods, the Grandmother Spruces, the Ocean and the Living World. To the turn of a word.

Especially to my maternal grandparents who were most like parents to me, my daughter *Che-ge-mem we'-yon* who taught me what it is to really love and my daughter who is in the Spirit World who taught me that there is no such thing as death;

To my cousin *Worth Many Fishes*, my mentors *John G., Ken N.* and *Terri B.*, my dear friends *B, D & M*, my basket teacher *The Pretty One, Kathy* and *Joseph* who cared enough to fight for what was right, and my hero *Joe Gio.* for their unconditional love and support; You altered the course of my life.

Thank you for whispering words to me and giving my life dimension. My wish is to have honored you all. May you find truth among the pages.

In memory of Puppy who was always in the middle of this book. Thank you for the joy you brought our lives.

CONTENTS

[13]

FOREWORD:

This book is born of connecting ideas, dreams, and events that have occurred to point me toward this collection of words that can be called *poetics*.

My Grandmother encouraged me to start writing before I was thirteen years old as a way to cope with the world around us. I later went on to college in order to understand the "language of the enemy" (Harjo, Bird, Blanco & Cuthand), and found that there is a lot of disjuncture in the general population because we are not all speaking the same language, sometimes not even within our own families. My work is an expression of spirit, philosophy, and culture as well as experience from working in the field of social work. Through creative writing, I hope to open windows and doors to other worlds and concepts by identifying commonalities in art, emotions, and experiences.

My Grandmother was known for having dreams that came true. Once in my youth, she shared a dream where she said I presented myself in her bedroom (some 80 miles away) spouting the words of an unwritten poem. All that she could remember were the words, *"cast in darkness, dark-fired for beauty"*. Over the years, I tried to incorporate those words into my writing hoping to somehow time-travel, until life became too distracting and I forgot that moment in time. Just after my Grandmother's death (some 28 years later), my teenage daughter went to live with my mother. In these difficult moments, I recalled the words that my Grandmother said I would come to write and took up poetry again. After I wrote the first poem in this book, in order to honor her and her many lessons, a pile of papers was found in my Grandmother's bureau and a written note on torn paper said,

"write me a book".

1 *Koh-toks*

'Oo'
(To Exist)

THE EDGE OF THE CONTINENT

At the edge of the continent
where the horizon holds the keys to answers,
time and tide wait for no man
until the filter of life sheds
to reveal the edge of time
where reality simply exists,
expressionless.

In that place,
as the waves of time recede,
gems of understanding are revealed,
glistening like agates,
telling the tale of a life
constructed.

Cast in darkness, dark-fired for beauty,
journey's end reveals an evolution of soul,
pain converted to love,
a life genuinely
expressed.

Should pain then be tempered in life,
distractions ignored,
torn hearts not repaired,
when that which brings tears
was destined to ignite us
and band us
with all generations?

We are not just our bodies;
We are interconnected with everything,
and yet we are nothingness;
We are stardust ~
born to remember
who we are.

Transcend the patterns of suffering
and honor the crystallization of love.
Peel away the wealth earned in life,
live for the firing of the soul;
Live for love on the other side of pain.

WALLFLOWER

Do you see me for the beauty I am?
A pale rose blowing in the wind?
A kind heart?
Beautiful eyes?
An attentive approach?

I laugh. I breathe.
I think.
I have the same wants and needs as my sisters.
I am a person first.
What about me stands out from the bouquet?

I have dreamed you
and you have dreamed me.
I know you in this other reality.
You meet my eyes across the room
and I know you remember this.

When I breathed you in,
I held your essence inside me,

[25]

like a golden blue sunrise; Like hope;
The memory of you still fills my heart.
Your eyes tell me you know what I know.

Yet, you say you are waiting for the girl of your dreams;
You say you *like what you like*;
How can I find myself within your definition?
Would it matter if you knew I was nobility
or a personality on T.V.?

Why not me?

All we can hope to have in this world is kindness.
If we're not meant to be,
at least I can carry the thought of you
in my heart.

Before you go,
whisper to me what it takes to catch the eye.
Should I be airbrushed or plastic?
What type of connection is real anymore?
Maybe love is not magic and just has to grow.

BOARD GAME

Players set around the game,
poker faces, eager to be the champion.
Who will have the skill to tromp the competitors?

Round-and-round the board they go
spiraling into a heated frenzy
to gather money and keep others from it.

Like windows that open up to the players' true selves,
glimpses of personality are seen
as people disengage from their preferred facade.

Emerging from the depths of their beliefs
comes true character, worldview and personality:
a sore loser, a manipulator, and more.

Parts of behavior, perhaps of the wounded soul within,
the skills of maturity now pulled back,
interacting according to a basic nature;

With *either/or* choices,
in-groups develop and certain people are cast out,
the benefactors not wanting to disrupt their comfort.

Look closely because the curtains will draw closed
as "*it was just a game*",
yet peeks out of the window to be seen again later.

So very protective of this inner core,
when will the window ever open
to allow in healthy and fresh ways of being?

...with the player that is ostracized from the game,
who engages in inclusive activities,
modeling a different way to engage in life.

MODERN BURDEN BASKET

Sweet little girl
blossoming into a beautiful young woman,
slight and graceful,
intelligent and witty,
who wouldn't admire the treasure?

Can she comply with the role assigned
and agree to be kept down
or face family disownment;
Exile?

Left to bear the burden of chores
and raise the children herself;
War wounds develop in her appearance
as youth fades;

She falls from her pedestal.

Objectified as a symbol of distaste,
the treasure is now scorned, *fool's gold,*
even though she was not taught about her value
or given the tools to survive alone.

Her choices are to remain infantile
or become a cougar.

County files are assigned by *her* name.
If something is wrong in the family, it is *her* fault.
If the man has left, *she* was not worthy.
If her new relationship is married already,
that too is *her* indiscretion.

What other journey would have resulted in less bleeding?
What clarity of path was needed?
Her life, a collection of pain.

Society reinforcing woman as the burden bearer,
a modern day distortion.

PARENTING OURSELVES

We shared the same window to the world.
Each seeing life with different eyes,
each with a natal wound; Unwanted.
We clung to the parent who had feelings.

It was not enough to want a parent.
It was not enough that someone cared.
We needed guidance and respect,
tolerance, resources and networks.

Shaking to our bones, we were tossed around like objects;
Made to fight each other,
cut off from the world,
as if we were bred to be entertainment.

How would we come to stand on our own,
sorted out depending upon favor
or expectation
and role?

Pulling ourselves up from
the broken bootstraps of our father,
only as adults, we developed value.
Yet we are so far behind, we are no prize.

Separate from each other, blaming and angry;
What does it matter that you never see your sibling,
you see the world differently anyway
or...do you?

Talking stopped when survival was the name of the game.
All we remember is a child's perspective
of how one was favored, the others behaving badly.
What trust was received in order to give?

Is all we have in common - grief?

For the love of the loss we had together,
for the shared blood and destiny,
could we not even take a moment to say,

"I don't want to talk about it, but I just want to love you"?

POLITICS

Thrill-kill Warrior,
who stalks you, unseen,
while you hunt others for joy?

You strike on multiple levels:
coercion, cornering, undermining,
unable to fill your gluttonous soul.

But a shadow haunts your path,
created by your own disconnect;
Your deeds will not go unpaid.

People will serve you or love you
or you'll take their job away,
force them into relationship.

[30]

Many weapons you will use:
charm, language, privilege,
threats of removal or court action.

Your personal devil grows stronger,
no longer smoke but a reflection
in your mirror.

You carry a deep wound in your heart
that has grown into infection -
everything you touch becomes sickness.

Purposefully manipulating environments,
orchestrating actors around you,
a real circus drama;

How many spirits will you try to break,
evidence precariously constructed,
consuming the world around you?

You can never cover all your tracks
and while you focus on hunting,
you are stalking yourself.

You grow weary of fighting yourself,
poison eating at your flesh
until your own devil kills you.

CHAH-CHEW

For the fight of my life,
I've a weathered face
and strong mitts for hands.

Born to a family who survived genocide
with no interventions
before life reached me,

every intimate relationship,
dangerous or abusive;
How am I supposed to react?

Drowning. Fighting. An uphill struggle.
Teachers dismiss me. Peers shun me.
I am American *Indian*.

My inheritance is stress,
destined for health problems,
there is so much loss in my life.

They killed most of my relatives up at Redwood Creek -
the survivor became a child slave
until she would be married off young;

Introduction
into the family dynamic
that women are not valuable;

It was the era
of *Indian* scalps
for 25 cents apiece.

It is just like I was there.
I know these truths in my blood,
an inherited memory.

I am angry because it keeps me alive.
I know what is real
and it's not the things they teach in school.

My battle scars are badges of honor.
Life wears at me,
but I've earned a place of wisdom.

I fight daily.

GLORY HUNTER

Olive skin and dark eyes,
a beautiful son of your People,
a modern day angel;

You smiled your way into status
so you would be honored with access
to dig ancient remains.

Just like the anthropologists of old,
you make assumptions, piece together unrelated parts
and glue them with fairytales.

Guesswork becomes fact
because your name
is attached;

You are so lost from your own People,
you seek truth
in the artifacts of others.

Like Kroeber[1],
traditional People laugh
at your kind,

who disrespected us
so we made up stories
every time he asked.

You have been trained
to be a fraud;
You need to go find yourself;

Trust your skills,
you will find the way there,
uncover the truths of your own past.

---

[1] A.L Kroeber was a 1900's anthropologist who would often visit my
relatives and ask them repeatedly for their stories, a practice that
unfortunately continues to this day. The Elders grew tired of this
disrespectful behavior and started making up stories to get this visitor to
go away. Kroeber assessed the Yurok people as "being incapable of
developing tales" and even being "anally fixated", (Kroeber, A.L.
(1976). *Yurok Myths*. University of CA Press: Berkeley) not realizing
that he was actually the *butt of the jokes*.

[34]

URBAN VISION QUEST

I am paper-thin,
away from my own country;
Green trees and grey buildings out of focus,
I see only shadows, not the light.

Dreams and reality melt into one;
One following the other,
as if time doesn't matter.
I wander empty streets, walking between worlds.

Everyone I meet is a guide, sent to influence direction;
People who exist in one reality
may look differently in Dreamtime
or not exist at all.

Needing to remember that not everyone
sees the Spirit World
and to take care not to slip and reveal
their secrets,

I laugh and label what I know as *psychic*
but I am alone -
a wanderer on a solitaire journey
that only makes sense over time.

Only pain or fear, thirst or hunger
seem to connect me to the *Good Road*
where the world is peeled back
and the truth is visible.

Only then do the gifts of the Creator
become clear
and I am thankful to be chosen -
to carry the burden.

[35]

SPIRIT KEEPER

There she sat on her forty-year old furniture,
playing solitaire,
slowly sipping thick coffee,
contemplating all the moves ahead.

The dark surrounded the cabin,
pressing in on the window glass,
wild animals stirred outside,
it was eerily quiet on the South Bank Road.

Her hair was crazy-wild,
salt-and-pepper grey,
curling down her shoulders;
It was as if a wind stirred about her.

At work during the day,
neat as a pin and grandmotherly sweet,
she put on her apron
and welcomed guests....

Open by Chance
the antique shop attracted all kinds,
buyers, sellers, mountain men;
She loved to see them all.

Year by year, she learned family trees and networks,
constructed lives and manipulated dreams,
an expert on the stars;
Playing out all considerations.

No one knew
she was the *Center of the World*,
a presence to be reckoned with -
holding everyone's numbers.

[36]

If she tugged one
and pushed another into place,
after awhile the relationships took what was provided
to them and grew on their own.

She knew that words,
like germs,
can be introduced into any environment
and grow in their Petri dish.

Quietly, she knew that the follower, or even the observer,
influences the leader,
and without notice,
changes the environment.

Mysterious brown eyes
with blue rims,
a narcissistic empress,
left over from the time of royalty,

she knew that confidence
eliminates question of authority
and that the poor
have nothing.

In her time,
where she had little choices,
her best friend became her deck of cards,
windows to souls.

RESILIENCE

Medicine Song went on a trip,
sold for food
and pain killers,
bound for the Smithsonian.

Dance regalia,
the wealth of the family,
disappeared
on a train.

Someone used up all the Luck
wishing for the world to be right again
and there was no way
to find peace.

Our relatives were killed
and left for dead,
hunted for pocket change;
Children taken for slaves.

Why did this happen?
How did the world get turned upside down
when holding these treasures
meant we were living life right?

Why are Outsiders
always looking to see our resilience
when we're *set up* to see how tough we can be
and we're tired of not doing well?!?

Did we die
and then the world become sick?
Did our DNA^2 dilute?
Why can't we stop the clear cutting of our world?

Werrp'
remembers the truth
even though
parents are not available.

Finding the way home
over generations,
never taught culture,
Butterfly has not been *conquered.*

It's all about a journey,
and being reborn to know what's really important...
that it may not look the same as yesterday,
but to keep on living.

(Note - Studies on the Monarch Butterfly have found that seven
generations after migrating from home, the next generations return home
without ever knowing their ancestors).

---

^{2} *Genome Project* findings support the long known fact that race is a
construct, that in fact, there is no dilution of DNA (deoxyribonucleic
acid) through the generations because each person inherits a full set from
each parent. At one time, Federal Indian Policy set in motion the rules
for who would be considered *Indian* by assigning quantums to
descendants, with the intent that at some point in time, there would be no
Indians left due to intermarriages and thereby no longer a Trust
responsibility owed. (Please refer to *Recommended Readings* under
Indexes for more information on these topics).

RECIPE

At River's edge where the wind takes my prayer,
I shake my hair loose,
the words of my mind cast adrift,
like pheromones.

My heartbeat,
the drum that shakes the earth;
My voice starts at the depths of my soul,
changing the vibration of my cells.

I become one with the world.

Across time and distance,
dream or waking place,
I saturate my spirit,
repeating the song,
calling it to come to life.

My flesh snaps with electricity,
organs withdraw,
for my body to take over
as a tuning fork.

I become *my will*.

I am no witch.
The words must be the Creator's,
in balance with goodness,
speaking the others' same heart language.

For magic to happen,
there must be agreement,
the elements in harmony with my song;
A net that has been cast for those seeking the same direction.

[40]

A FACE OF PARANOIA

Genocide imbedded fear in your cells,
passed along in subtle interrelations
either implied by absence of interaction
or expressed directly;

Institutions reinforce your beliefs,
through labels
and denial of equal benefits,
visual images, song and print;

It must be true,
that you are inherently bad,
that *people are out to get you*;
Steel your heart for safety.

You trust no one
because no one has given you cause,
you believe those close to you
will sell you out to stop their own pain;

Afraid to step outside,
crime statistics are up;
Fear drives you to be critical.
You become crafty in order to survive.

Can't you just shut yourself in?
The neighbor threatens to sue you,
so you avoid *that side* of the house,
even though you were the trespasser;

You shorten the continuum of possibilities
by seeing everything in black or white categories;
Moving from 0 - 60 mph in a flash,
"either you are for me or against me..."

[41]

But *no one knows* what you're thinking.

People around you are so emotional themselves;
Don't they see how much hurt you carry?
Does no one care about *you*?
You can't trust to that, **ever.**

Instead of being more inclusive of your family,
you separate them out,
throw away the key,
call for reinforcements if they come by.

You justify your actions,
distort words to fit your own plot,
pass the fairytale along hoping others will believe you.
The more dramatic the story,
the more *help* people will consider you need.

Except what you have done
is reinforce fear and disrespect and pass along genocide,
denying more people their opportunity for love;
Outsiders minimizing your pain as *dramatic*.

Your descendants now doomed
to repeat the same pattern into the future
when you are not around to suffer their consequences;
Perfectly role-modeled;

But nothing matters now
except the instant gratification of anger
and being able to lock Oneself up,
safe from the outside world.

There is no *Happily Ever After*,
because you made sure of that.

[42]

TIME

Born into contractions,
life is measured quickly;
Heartbeats counting the time;

Slowing with age,
measuring time now by clocks
and universal calendars;

Growing pains contract around us,
moving at a slower rate,
sometimes heard as the pulse of a radio song;

Day in, day out,
waxing and waning,
the wing-beats of life;

Developmentally seen as holidays
and events, sometimes
by the change of season;

Puberty shortens the contractions
as they come faster again,
a beat racing to advance into adulthood;

Always measured by the throb of contraction:
growth spurts, menstruation, anger, brain cycles,
recessions, digestion, intercourse, friendships,
illness, birth, menopause...

then life slows again
as we transition into older age,
breathing in and breathing out...

[43]

sometimes life is measured by the end of projects,
or Divine Justice that does not come in our time,
though we wait on bated breath;

Measuring our steps on this plane,
more like the tides coming in now,
ebb and flow....

We are enveloped in the
contractions of a universal
heartbeat,

counting time
with our experience of life,
each clock measuring differently.

BLANK SLATE

Emotions, suffering, criticism,
anger, bad words...

all flowing
through me,
their filter,
and I can love the person without judgment
or attachment,
helping sort through
what matters to them,
being present in the moment...

except for the things
that hook up on my own heart strings,
those things I can't let go of myself,
my pain.

Then I am no longer a guide,
my counsel tainted -
I become the needy
if I am unable
to recognize my limitations,
my humanness;
Unable to clearly see the situation,
coloring the story with my own,
making leaps in judgment,
distorting the truth;

Yet moving through
this realization,
if I do not use you
to fix it,

I become
stronger,
more
compassionate.

ROMANCE NOVEL

Just like a novel,
suspense constructed
for your amusement,
the excitement of the audience;

You captured a relationship,
reduced it to its essence,
keeping small memories of disdain,
shedding all the rest;

You catch your breath,
because you are wanted,
by those who have cornered you,
unwanted by those that flee from your destruction;

You orchestrate your father coming to the rescue,
although he has never been in your life before;
Your uncles stand like sentries to your virtue,
but you know the back door around them while they aren't
looking;

Everyone is your puppet,
each character flaw, you provide;
But where is the foundation for the values
so that there can be a meaningful plot?

Fantasizing about how people suffer away from you
or what you will do if you have to face them again;
Embraced by the ones who do you most harm,
you are safe with your captors in their sterile environment.

Empowered that you can script such a drama
all evolving around you;
You can have anything your way,
but do you really know what that is?

The pen belonging to someone else,
whispering words in your ear,
hearing someone else's story and idea of love;
Serving someone else's purpose or anger;

Bound to the bindings of your story,
the pages deteriorate and age,
you are limited to that one dimension
while life goes on around you.

PARTY'S OVER

My heart is eroding.
What is the cost
to numb the pain?

Booze and meth are fun;
My parents knew this.
All I ever wanted was to reach 21 so I could play too.

Happy.

Now that I am here,
the parties are like cyclones,
sucking out my insides.

My relationships are like fires
and I'm standing in the house
watching it all blow down.

The hospital gave me a month to live.
I will miss the drama
of coughing up blood...

Fighting has been fun,
an endless parade of comedy;
Now at the end,
my friends and family only come by
to steal from me;

Angry.

I lived life to the fullest,
at least as much as I could handle.
My children don't know me.
My parents abandoned me.

[47]

I could have been an actor,
a doctor,
or an *Indian* Chief.

I chose to be
a Party *Warrior*;
I never wanted to face reality.

I don't care about the bills I leave behind.
I do remember names even though I pretend not.
It's easier to slip away and die.

Sad.

Someone needs to clean up the mess
when I'm away.
Ask one of my hallucinations.

So tired.

TREATY

So where do we arrive at
when there is no truce,
each believing that their story
is the version that should be believed?

Hurt feelings,
egos attached to outcomes?
Is there ever a place to
go forward?

Maybe turmoil is an addiction
or one side benefits in some way,
but at what price
to always be at war?

There could be agreement
that the past is history,
that casualties were suffered,
and that no one has won,

why not
go forward
by agreeing that there is disagreement,
individual differences?

...finding common ground
to mutual understanding of what *words* mean
to eliminate any emotional triggers
or assumptions?

But how are oozing wounds dressed
after so many bridges have been set ablaze?
Perhaps by establishing safe boundaries,
and rules to healthy fighting;

By rising above differences in understanding
and realizing your enemy is a reflection of you
coming from another place of humanity;
Love seen despite privilege, jealousy,
guilt, unequal benefits;

Each threshold of understanding
reached together
by building trust in mutual experience,
a little at a time;

Upon conflict,
gently asking for clarification
or purpose without judgment;
Each view point valid.

Every opinion,
skill-set, experience, belief,
a necessary part
to the healthy whole;

There is a place for everyone
despite where that may be
as viewed by another;
Respecting ebb and flow;

It is beyond the contest
of right or wrong,
Loser or Winner,
only how each contributes;

A peace beyond the immediate;
A spiritual win,
behind each door to the soul,
a triumph to the brevity of life.

Learn to separate out your emotion
for the business at hand
and deal with what you can;
The rest will come in time

...with love held in common.

[51]

DAYDREAMER

Caught between two worlds
like a twig in the current,
succumbing to the river around you;

Do you exist here
...or there?

Wake up Dreamer!
Your life is passing you by.

Learn the current
so you can understand the times -
and when it is okay just to float along.

If you get wedged, stuck along the way,
you can dream only as long as
it takes to decay.

Shake off being numb with fear!
Wake up and join life!

Your spirit is being stolen away.

4 SALMON

It is easier to loosen relationship connections
if *hate* is introduced;
Same tactics of war applied
internally in the family.

Why does *respect* have to be earned
when all life is deserved of acknowledgement?
Unless you need to hurt something to feel better,
learning disrespect has to be encouraged.

One must look beyond personal desires
and see the other side of the story,
even the story not taught;
Secrets protecting lies.

Maybe the fighter is actually the defender
or the villain is just demonized
because someone else benefits;
The victim victimized?

Mutation occurs when
a garbage dump is created
yet noses turn up at the creation
unable to face the responsibility and choices.

What you treat with
disrespect,
reflects
back to you;

I won't engage in your game.
I follow a different purpose.
I will always take the high road
and let your behaviors fall by the wayside.

You may steal my property
and label me a *bad character*,
teach my children disrespect,
run up my bills or destroy my car;

This does not diminish the truth
nor change my life's course;
When tested,
I will still pray that 4 fish find you.

(Note - The reference to fish is equivalent to wealth and good health.)

SELF EVIDENT

Don't hate me because of who I am.
We each have a life course
with challenges and benefits;
Your perception of over-abundance is *only that*.

I was not created for you,
to meet your needs,
so if I don't respond as you predict,
it has nothing to do with you.

I measure my path by how I walk it;
I do not tend to what you are doing.
When you interfere with my way,
you only add to your burden.

Life eventually finds balance;
Goodness is met with adversity
to even out the essence...
so don't tip the scale,

you are not strong enough
for this spiritual debt
and you show *your tell*
by acting on your weakness.

My life's work speaks for itself,
what does your path reveal?
By being negatively vested in me,
it reveals immaturity, jealousy, poverty.

I continue on my way
regardless of you,
my deeds
a window to my values.

[55]

WORTH

I am more than the damage done to my body.
I am more than my job, profession or degree.
I am more than my family of origin or creation.
I am more than the sum of my parts.
I am more than what people would say about me.
I am more than my pocketbook or tax base.

I am more than...
...my age, my gender, my blood type;
...my talents;
...my role;
...my grade point average;
...my intelligence;
...what I say or don't say;
...my possessions;
...the friends or enemies that I keep;
...my attributes;
...my risk factors;
...my medical chart;
...my case file;
...my court file;
...my intentions and dreams;
...my surname;
...my life insurance policy;
...my bruises;
...my place on your likeability scale[3];
...my death.

How do you see me?

---

[3] Reysen, S. (2005). Construction of a new scale: The Reysen likeability scale. Journal of *social behavior and personality.*

DEPARTING

Where do *suicide notes* go
when a person leaves this world?
...Hiding in a dark box, burned,
thrown away?

What instructions do you leave for those who will read?
What values did you hold dear?
What is it to make *a mark* in the world,
when over time, it is forgotten, nothing preserved?

The thoughts that caused disruption to life,
do they transfer over to the Afterlife?
Is there then distortion in your
cosmic pattern?

What good does it do to advance
in civilization
if it doesn't matter in the end;
People losing sight of goodness?

Romanticizing who will care,
who will treasure the note,
who will have a tear in their heart
for the act;

Everyone will be stunned
and stop time to think of this -
Is that what you wanted?
What is the reason you existed in the first place?

What if there was no construct
to the definition of death,
for in life, there was never any meaning -
no time taken to build love?

Be more than your life
before your days disappear.
Once you are gone,
the only spirit remaining are the words
you leave behind.

DREAM OF A DREAM

Overwhelmed with joy,
it is hard to imagine
that love could be real;

Caught in the night in a net of love,
burdened with passion's song,
we cloak our daytime portraits with sleep;

Swept in the tides of unconsciousness,
we are blind that the truth *simply is*;
There follows no noun... adjectives fall away;

We are carried to another horizon,
an Eden where there is no worry,
sharing the same stars:

A tender kiss,
held so close
that we share the same breath;

The initial light of life that attracted us
becomes a healing tool,
the truth so basic.

Destiny dreams us regardless of the miles;

Inviting you to peel away your eyes,
give your ears a voice,
listen to the River with your soul.

With a moonlit beach to pour out our hearts,
a silver forest in which to dance,
a choir of amphibians for our amusement;

I awake from these dreams painted across the night sky;
I only need remove the memories
to begin breathing again.

DISTINCTIONS & CONSIDERATIONS

important business meeting vs. pow wow;
getting ready for battle vs. putting on war paint;
reasonable efforts vs. active efforts;
directive strategies vs. reflective strategies;
naming vs. exploring vs. labeling;
evil vs. psychologically fragile vs. fear economy;
borderline behavior vs. learned behavior;
rely vs. depend vs. trust vs. need;
reservation vs. rez;
duty vs. rape;

forgiveness vs. payment vs. releasing of energy vs.
reconciliation vs. surrender vs. diminished;

hostile environment vs. low intensity warfare vs.
power struggle vs. domain building;

crazy vs. trauma;
chief vs. honored elected leader;
dance leader vs. human being;
lack of language vs. discipline vs. abuse vs. poor skills;
extra cars in the yard vs. extra car parts when needed;
dependent vs. independent vs. interdependent;

concretization vs. confirmation bias vs. reification vs.
self fulfilling prophecy;

rumination vs. talk too much vs. words without meaning vs.
trade language;

truth vs. truths vs. historic truth vs. reality vs.
cultural truth vs. adjudicated truth vs. convenience;

[60]

DSM vs. fluctuating constructs and realities vs.
ideological vs. societal beliefs vs. actuality;

dialectical vs. dialogical;
performance issue vs. training issue vs. hostile environment;
choice vs. impulse vs. behavior;
martyr vs. scapegoat vs. favorites;
poor vs. crazy;
colonialism vs. discrimination vs. prejudice vs. racism;
childish vs. child-like vs. childhood;
identity vs. inferiority;
legitimized vs. delegitimized vs. illegitimate;
truancy vs. transportation;
drift vs. power shuffle;
disloyal vs. disagreeable vs. disappointment;
impossible vs. impractical;
student vs. scholar;
spectrum vs. continuum vs. category;
personal myth vs. myth vs. rumor vs. denial vs. strategy;

antisocial vs. psychopath vs. sociopath vs. socially distinct
vs. cluster of issues;

acknowledgement vs. apology vs. accountability;
melting pot vs. distinct groups together;
ignorance vs. violence vs. lack of language skills;
honesty vs. boundaries;

First Nations vs. American Indian vs. Native American vs.
People vs. just people;

embellish vs. generalize vs. distortion vs. language skill;

angry vs. overwhelmed vs. lack of language vs. voiceless vs.
loud vs. fear vs. helpless;

[61]

criminal activity vs. gathering for sustenance/religious
reasons;

drug abuse vs. drug use vs. escapism;
racist vs. institutional racism;
conquered vs. broken treaties;
name vs. definition;
labels vs. process;
schizophrenia vs. ammonia level vs. mimic;
signature goes here vs. signature stolen;
avoiding eye contact vs. not wanting soul stolen;
absolutes vs. poor critical thinking vs. lack of language;

yelling vs. needing to be heard vs. guilt vs. disability vs.
acculturation vs. fear;

ADHD vs. sugar imbalance vs. child abuse symptom;
tolerance vs. respect;

legal constraints vs. release of information vs. out to get me;

smart vs. applied knowledge;

looking vs. being respectful vs. flirting vs. being mindful of
the environment;

risk vs. privilege;
paranoid vs. realistic vs. confirmation bias;
fenced backyard vs. the world as a backyard;
judgment vs. listening;
family (nuclear) vs. family (extended);

fighting vs. panic disorder vs. exhibiting anger vs. being a
warrior;

domestic violence vs. parental alienation vs. parental
interference vs. rescuing vs. kidnapping;

behavior problem vs. responding to environment;
legitimizing vs. building vs. demolition;
assimilated vs. acculturated;
superstar vs. standard;
tool vs. weapon;
weird vs. character;
discipline vs. shame;
criticism vs. self hatred;
chaos vs. internalized oppression;
puppet vs. master;

blame vs. responsibility vs. accountability vs. careful vs.
resolution;

political party vs. extremism vs. belief system vs.
generalization;

can't vs. won't vs. don't vs. shouldn't;
unseen vs. seen vs. physical vs. metaphysical;

knowing vs. believing vs. thinking vs. experiencing vs.
assuming vs. feeling vs. seeing vs. pathologizing;

rights vs. privileges;
fast vs. well;
us vs. them;
descendant vs. neither here nor there;

defiance vs. oppositional vs. protection vs. protest vs.
disrespect vs. survival;

secrets vs. privacy vs. rumors vs. maintaining confidentiality vs. denials vs. deceit vs. myth building vs. asking for help;

delay vs. development vs. attuned vs. challenged vs. worldview vs. diagnoses vs. privilege vs. multi-cultural;

desire vs. choice;
I am vs. I am of you vs. I-it vs. I-thou vs. I-you vs. It-world[4];
competition vs. compassion;
fight vs. flight vs. decompensation;
meanness vs. integrity vs. all that in-between;
joining vs. splitting vs. lying;

delayed vs. unaware vs. perception vs. acculturation vs. misunderstood vs. misinformed vs. uneducated vs. misspoken vs. misdiagnosed vs. inconsistency vs. fearful vs. story vs. attention getting behavior vs. embarrassment vs. diminishment vs. being private vs. agenda vs. brainwashing vs. manipulation vs. lack of language skill vs. contradiction vs. irregularity vs. both/and vs. **lie**....

(Note - vs. or *versus* is intended to invoke consideration of the differences between the terms which are sometimes considered interchangeable, but can be a completely different thing. At times, words that belong on a continuum are split by the term versus.)

---

[4] Buber, Martin. *I and Thou.* Translated by Ronald Gregor Smith. New York: Charles Scribner's Sons, 1958

ADDICT

Rewards versus punishments;
Reinforced from the groups involved
or looking in from the outside;
Addicted to power, entertainment,
aggression, panic, reactions, imagination;
Drama, name-dropping, fame, hurting others;
Food, romance, computer games, parties;
Seeking comfort, warmth,
things lacking from childhood;
Internal chemicals,
external stimulants;
High on life;
High on emotion;
High on negative or positive energy;
Life is a wonderland of drugs
but sometimes with not many alternatives;
A person first.

SACRIFICE

Does the sickness in the home belong
to the one who distorts the truth,
making excuses for people
who never learn from their mistakes
because they never know what is wrong
which results in others
being angry because they were then
cheated of a voice and felt there was no justice,
all for the sake of no conflict in the moment?

OR, could it be the person
whose own life is so desperate,
that someone else has to be targeted

as the failure, the bad or sick one,
in order to bring attention or glory
to the one creating stories, the Martyr?

Perhaps once anger is uncovered;
Despair and anguish removed,
sacrifice is only dust
covering up the sickness in the rubble,

the cover story now gone and the real foundation revealed.

RAGE

You weren't traveling along
at my speed
when I came upon you;

Why do you race me now?

Non-driver!
You have your ego on the road!

I am on my own
race-course,
with a different goal in life;
You risk our lives
when you cut me off,
no one gets educated
from your choices.
You cross over to an act of evil,
when you abuse your power.
You are not responsible for me
and I am not responsible for you.
I am not judging that your urgency
is less important than mine,

[66]

but how do *you* know?
And why would you interfere?
You only demonstrate lack of control....

And I can see that I have triggered something else in you;
Some pain festering underneath your reaction;
Perhaps evidence that you lack self-efficacy elsewhere.

HOUSE OF CHAOS

Parents as portholes
through which everything must pass;
Behavior around you falls into predictable patterns;

Unsettled, unable to bond,
what choices are left the children of chaos
but hyper-awareness, hyper-reactions, hyper-behavior?

Demonstrating behavior at school:
drug use, plucking out eyelashes, disobedience,
fighting or self harm;

Hello!
Does anyone see me?!?
How about now!?

A home built from a deck of cards,
everything frantically pieced together for stability,
ready to blow over at any moment;

Adversity becomes a gift,
the means
to achieve a Divine Purpose.

[67]

Negativity gouges in your side,
you feel that you can do
no *right*;

What is learned when the truth is hidden?
When feelings are stifled,
anger becomes the language of the family.

Truth is perspective
but you are
kept from the light;

Blamed for what you don't know
to bear the burden
of others' pain;

Your sacrifice
will have meaning
over time;

Good or bad
is irrelevant.
Forgiveness, the only peace.

TIMELESS

Time has raced by.
I don't feel the age of my body
except as measured by death around me.

I am as young as I ever was,
with the wisdom of time to mark age,
but the same feelings as youth.

I hear old men speak as if they were lovesick,
all of our spirits
timeless.

I dream of my childhood
and see magic;
I remember *play* as if it were yesterday.

Age has only been an awakening of things around me,
the weight of knowledge
holding my body back.

Sometimes I stand in the mirror
and look at the mirror behind,
combing reflections for that other reality.

How many possibilities did I miss
because I moved too fast,
or didn't move at all?

On the other side of the stars,
when I dream eternal,
will *Time* follow?

YOUTH

Loved and comforted,
cared for with no wants,
grown to be self-assured;

Smart and energetic,
no fear of harm;
Indestructible;

The pride of the family,
beauty and strength,
fierce willfulness;

Should your path have been more painful
to temper your power?
Humility to provide you with grace?

What lessons must you now face -
to know that poverty is a slaver,
that love only accomplishes so much?

Will you know to plan for a future?
Did you hear the lessons you were taught?
Do you know to watch for hidden agendas?

Did we fail by loving you
so much,
Descendant of War?

Can you respect the sacrifices made
so you could thrive,
or will you become a *Master Manipulator*?

Find direction,
know that life is about moments;
Do not repeat historic mistakes.

Reality created in each conversation;
Find the thing that lights you up
and apply it to whatever you do.

Be kind.

KALIEDESCOPE

Life has been a shattering of glass for you;
So painful, the only way to view it,
through a pretty Kaleidoscope.

With this filter on reality,
you can remain numb,
and not walk on glass to the other side of truth.

When you don't like the view,
you only have to shake the pieces up,
and see something slightly different;

Fill in the blanks with what might have happened
from the time you start
until the pieces settle.

Can't bear to remember your part in history
or hear what others are saying now,
just shake the colors again.

Distortion of reality
makes your life happier
and blurs the lines enough not to carry responsibility.

How long will you hide inside of this looking glass?
Will you continue to disown those
who don't share your world?
Simply turn the glass once more.

When you are ready,
the larger world has much brighter colors,
and you can keep safe by creating your own boundaries...

,,,so no one will ever create chaos for you again.

[71]

NO PLACE FOR ME

At night I wander aimlessly
down darkened blue streets,
empty and still.

I pass through manicured yards
of dark emerald greens;
Windows of amber light translate to safety.

Always having to move,
never safe for a moment; Unwanted;
I become Spirit to survive.

Through houses I wander,
room to room, uninhibited,
accessing places not available during the day.

Each place connected by a window, door, or closet.
I have to be creative,
sometimes moving down the hallway, behind the world.

Through deserted alleys,
and magnificently carpeted abandoned highways,
running or seeking, I don't know.

There's always a way out,
another world to explore;
A means to walk into your dreams.

I find you by keeping an empty space in my heart
and calling for you to fill it.

Every room a rich adventure, a treasure;
I can stay as long as my needs are met...
but all I want to do is go home.

DISOWNED (another genocidal tool)

Exile.
Cast adrift.
Thrown away as an example:
Behave or die!

Torn family photos float in my wake.
Grandma's ashes cake the surface.
Home set ablaze at the shore.
My child kidnapped.

Hopeless against this tide.

What could I have done that was so bad?
I look out among the waves
and see others, also alone;

All women who once belonged to our family,
signs around their necks telling their story:
Homely. Tall. Educated. Outspoken.
Dramatic. Emotional. Bad Housekeeper. Different
Viewpoint. Barren. Loud. Menopausal.

Human.

...and right there we give over to the current,
floating without dignity or respect,
never once reaching out for another,
feeling worthless...

...the family's best chance at survival
removed
so *someone*
can exploit those left behind.

BEING

The Universe runs magic parallels through the heavens:
Each shooting star, an enchanting tear of happiness
trickling down my cheek;
Each black hole, the thirst of my lonely heart;

A constant melody flows through my mind,
weakened by my knowledge.
Its tune is not unknown to me,
it is love;

How like me everything is
dull or bright in its own context;
Each moon, my body;
Each particle of dust, a thought;

My love is an ever-running current;
My marrow,
babbling over time and space,
needy of all that it embodies;

Cruel it is that I am
such a being that I am all.
I may neither know more nor less;
I am alone.

FAMILY HERO

Asked to give up on life,
sacrifice so the family can survive,
but when you're gone, someone else will do;

[74]

Selected for your strength
and ability to fill the role,
you are reinforced for the job;

Every situation confirms what you're told:
It's all your fault,
don't you know you're *worthless?*

You're so *bad,*
the *Problem-Stirrer* in the house,
Drama-Queen, Scapegoat.

Why are you the way you are
when you're expected to take the abuse,
understand that degradation belongs to you?

Why can't you do better,
when love and resources are withdrawn,
when you're left excluded?

You'd still be isolated
if you hadn't run away,
good riddance Problem-Child!

While your family dynamic adjusts,
the silent treatment is the trigger,
the primal call to come home.

The world reacts
to the way you see yourself -
broken communication skills transfer over
to other environments.

Will you always see love as conflict?
Are you always the victim?
Are you injured enough that you bring *help* back home?

[75]

Quit complaining and do something!
Didn't you know that you were born to raise your parents?
That is why they cannot face their own blame.

Rise above your unresolved issues,
make something out of nothing and become everyone's hero,
but start with yourself first.

INDIAN ED

Great Uncle went to Boarding School
and learned that it wasn't okay to be *Indian*.
He brought this back to the family.

Grandmother passed it on to Mother,
who wanted the American dream.

She married Father who was racist,
and here I am with their blood in my veins.
A silent on-going war.

Isolated, abused, ignored while my parents' lives went on;
School was my refuge.

Still, in my world everything was a business transaction,
a Native concept Americanized:
I paid for my father's sins, my mother's lack of resources;
I paid for my younger sibling's actions.

The kindest words I heard were from teachers
who saw the littlest light inside, giving me hope.

Self efficacy.

Sanctuary.

Power.

A little warmth;

Time taken to guide me so I could hang on to life.

It still wasn't safe to be *Indian*,
but at least, it was an identity that I could fulfill.

(Note – At the time of this publishing, Native American students have
the highest drop-out rate among high school students based upon their
experiences with institutional racism, genocide, and worldview. Studies
demonstrate Native American students are disproportionately
overrepresented in this statistic. Indian Education was put in place to
support Native students after the Boarding School Era. Since its
inception, it has made a significant difference for several generations.)

KAY-GET

I am my Grandmother
and her relatives before her.

I am the spirit of Woman,
not unlike your wife.

I have chosen to be more than the gentle breeze,
succumbing to the weather around me.

I have power and precision,
dedication to have resolve.

I have earned the right to *own* my power,
triumphing over great odds to exist.

You find me sweet with a sharp edge,
eroticism in your eyes.

I am no sex-kitten,
nor do you interest me.

I am curious about things of depth
and interested in pursuing reality.

Ours was only a chance meeting
because Shallow Thinkers thought
an *Indian* should work with another *Indian*.

Do not delay me on my way,
your flattery and promises are rotten.

You cannot keep me nor afford me
and will pay for the insult.

I am full of life and wisdom.
I will not play your games.

You have tried to name me as your bride
and jeopardize the good work I do.

But you will find the source of my power
is beyond your pet name for me.

I reclaim that name as my right,
still untainted by you,

whom I leave behind,
slovenly and aging in your own gluttonous stench.

Paa' is the answer to your proposals,
forever and for the last time!

Go home to the woman you have taken,
learn respect.

(Note - My Grandmother had been called *Kay-get* after surviving a face
to face mountain lion encounter in (Quail's Valley) Hydesville,
California during the Great Depression.)

[79]

COAGULATION

It is said that the Old Ones
would collect the blood of the dead
in the event of a war,

and burn it with
all the person's unfinished business
left behind,

so as to free the soul
and not call it to return
and rejoin attachments.

Living and breathing as a collective
drawn to family if there is to be rebirth;
Our cosmic imprint.

Connected to each other and our environment,
as extensions of ourselves,
praying, living, dying, moving as a unit;

How real it is to feel the pull of Earth,
the rich depth beneath the feet,
the electricity of knowing place;

Everything is so alive,
a bond between us;
To be separate is exile;

What of it
when toxins invade
or clear cutting exists?

Like erosion
wearing at the flesh
or genocide to the family structure;

...now becoming thin and lifeless,
every blood cell reacting with a magnetic pull,
calling the drops all together.

Until the call of Spirit is heard,
and return to connectivity is possible,
loss of blood will quietly and methodically

...drain strength.

NOT A FOOTPRINT

No birthday.
No celebrations.
No photos.
No relationships.
No credit.
No voting.

Not traceable.
Not knowable.
Not rememberable.

Is there a reason to live?
Are we at the mercy of life's current?
How is our existence a Divine Expression?

No funeral.
No headstone.
No achievements in life.

If you have nothing,
then there is nothing to sacrifice,
so are we distracted from Divine Purpose?

Using relatives,
withdrawing from social activity,
selling off memories...

If we have no joy in life
and no markers to measure worth,
throwing away anything that changes the status quo,
then the Boarding School Era served its purpose.

CANARY IN THE MINE[5]

Bird in your cage,
why don't you breathe anymore?
Old Timers once listened to you.

Yes, there were always cries of injustice
but why couldn't you act more like everyone else?
Weren't you told that you should change your life,

even though you were in a cage,
with the Department of the Interior in charge of your fate;
Your resources stolen, not reimbursed, no apology?!

With the canaries gone,
who will speak for the rivers being sold to foreign nations
and stop the clear cutting of trees?

---

[5] *Canary in the Mine* refers to the practice of canaries being used in
mining to determine when there was no longer any oxygen left, with
their life or death being the signal. Native American *Indians* have often
been referred to as America's canaries.

[82]

What of it
that they built
the nuclear plant sitting on the earthquake fault?

Without you, who would know that preventive burning
keeps the spread of wild fires
or saving knaahl-koh might be important?
Who will notice that justice could be different, too?

When the last of your kind are dead,
and the air is gone,
who will sing for the rest left behind?

MIRROR, MIRROR

Who are you?
Who is in there?
What do you stand for?

Do you see your relatives?
Do they see you?
Do you know what you look like?

If you look long enough will you see
perfection or flaws,
or something else?

Are you disconnected enough
from this world
to fade into your reflection from other worlds?

Are you right with your deeds
so you can face yourself
in this life and others?

[83]

If you have everything you want,
do you still have yourself
or those you love?

When people see you,
do they hold feelings of love
or concerns for your behavior?

Do you look like you
or
like the people who raised you?

Does everyone see the same thing
or just the same people
who want you to be a certain way?

If you were to gift yourself anything,
would love be enough
or do you need to heal some pain

in order to become treasured?

SA-'A-WOR'

There are things set in motion,
meant to be,
every action or non-action
our life's journey, not our soul's journey.

You invited the role of martyr
so others would follow you,
pity you, care for you,
but it is an illusion to the choices you could make.

Shadow and shade,
it will fade,
created to manipulate your experience,
like baiting fish.

Inherent in this creation of a storm,
truth will burn through;
Lessons will be learned
regardless of environment or time.

Who will keep you in check
and temper your interactions?
You get what you want,
but it is transitory.

Distortion is irrelevant,
be it good or evil intent,
it too will dissipate
revealing accomplishment, not growth.

Are you so afraid of life,
to stand out in the sun?
Do you prefer the shade
in order to appear humble?

Do not live as a shadow of who you could be;
Become your true self.
Destiny may already be scripted,
but you can honor your path by simply being you.

COLLECTIVE MIND

I'm thinking,
you're saying,
he's dreaming,
we come together.

One conversation
coagulates
and other drops of words
are drawn.

Evolving collectively
in separate lives
as if
we lived as one.

He is she;
She is he;
There is no difference,
there is no boundary.

No developmental stages
among us,
only one season
we all weather.

Young or old,
our generational stories
become the same;
Every death, a loss for all.

The wisdom of the ages
becomes
the root
of our today.

[86]

Blood so strong
we know innately
what each other is thinking
as if we were there

across time,
and space,
forever
related.

It is pure magic
to *know*
how someone else
believes

so you can move
in tune
with their natural flow,
even at a distance.

If all this is true,
is it then betrayal
when One thinks
separately?

INDIAN WAY (a question)

Was it always the same
or has it changed
to match the environment?

Do we stagnate
and deteriorate
or do we grow with time?

Does *Indian Way*
mean no infrastructure,
isolation from the modern world?

Or is it adherence to tradition,
regardless of American laws;
Dual obligations?

Could it mean standing up for your family,
doing what is right,
regardless of sacrifice?

Does it have to mean
scorched-earth tactics,
destroying property; War?

Isn't it really about trusting
in a Divine Justice
which no one escapes?

Is being *Indian* just a hobby?
What are your ethics
When no one is looking?

When we forget the truth,
are we not forgetting
Indian Way?

Who interprets truth?
Is it them or us?
Does it have to be divisive?

Are we then assimilated?
Or are we dynamic enough to be
affluent in both worlds?

Do we have to fit a ready-made template?
Can there be more than
one *right* way?

UMBILICAL

Soul infusion,
anchored in birth,
destiny-bound to the creation,
a journey of Spirit;

Tethered to the dock of life,
attached by role,
by place and relationship,
in memory or beliefs;

The ability to survive
requiring endurance through rough seas
and heavy burdens
without taking on water;

Despite the degree of development,
each vessel must weather
its anchor's predisposition
to eventually find calm and forgiveness;

Drifting with the tide,
tacking between dependable resources,
finally arriving
at the port of self authentification;

A wise voyager learns to pull anchor,
shift direction,
securing a new lifeline
to the next stable environment;

Storms may pass by
but calm waters will return,
memories and miracles marking the way,
new ports to cling to;

After a lifetime of journey
when there are no longer any places to explore,
will you be strong enough to cut anchor
and trust yourself to the current?

VISITOR

Moth came for the holiday dinner
and hung around
to see how many pies were being served.

Gram said it was Great Grandfather
sent there to watch over us,
to check in on her before it was *her time*.

Another day, when times are tough,
chaos and desperation
fill the coffee cup,

Moth comes to visit;
Beautiful brown eyes on its wings,
caught in the car, unwilling to leave.

Returning later,
the visitor is dead,
still clinging to the parking token.

What message was to be conveyed?
Just delaying the car for a moment
or marking my thoughts at the time of arrival?

Who can advise me
when all of my Elders
are now departed?

There was purpose in these visits
reminding me
that we're always watched over.

NERR-MER-YEK'

Standing atop the jagged sea cliff
I toss my song out to the wind...
afraid for a moment...
then retrieve it unscathed.

I play with my song, sending it back out,
laughing with the freedom...
and as quickly as I cast it out,
I retrieve it.

Night comes to pass
and I dare sing once more.
You melt into my song and capture it
beneath my now-vacant eyes.

I look up into your face
and I cannot remove my desire.
You are the very night,
a deep and unashamed pureness.

As you hold my song in your hands,
silently stirring behind your back,
my soul yearns to teach you of love,
though of love I do not know myself.

I seep into your palms and through your heart
where interest first captured the warmth of your glance.
You add your own song
and we fall in love.

I clutch my heart and fall towards the surf
holding fast to your song.
I kiss the surface of death and rejoice -
I will not let this love leave me.

TO MY CHILD

I want to watch you grow into an adult.
I want to share in your life.
I want to reinforce boundaries so you feel safe,
and can know stability.

...to share your joys and triumphs.
...to have someone to talk to who has been there;
...someone to brace against in hard and frightening times;
...someone to sit back and let you
make independent choices safely;

I want to create memories together and not grow apart.
I want you to know your culture.
I want you to grow from your family stories...
and not be swallowed by them.

You need to understand that in this world,
people will charm you or criticize you
to believe in their agenda, their biases.
Power is *their* guiding light.

Question those who whisper stories,
there is always a motive, or two;
Not all things named *Truth*
include all perspectives, including yours.

It has not been easy,
not all choices popular;
My decisions different
for a purpose;

A removal of strife
so there was no struggle,
no prize
to fight over;

Do not judge your Elders
until you know the entire situation
as you were born into relationships
that existed long before you are ready to understand;

Separate out your feelings from your actions
and learn to be independent
of the political tides around you.
Learn the skills you will need to survive.

Sometimes you too will need to take a stand
for what you know is right even when it is painful,
but you can do it with kindness,
and it is never just *you against the world.*

Remember to give second chances
and keep yourself safe
by setting your boundaries
and respecting yourself.

Be kind to yourself
as you are only human;
Learn from your mistakes,
always seek out the whole story;

Treat others as you want to be treated;
Take responsibility for your choices;
Always remember
that there is more than one *right* way;

Forget me not.
I am more than the person who loves you;
I am you, older,
and your grandmother, younger.

Because of you, I've known love, and the pain of loving.
Because of you, I grew into an adult.
Because of you, I am whole.
Because of you, I was able to help others.

I have accepted that you will not remember
all the good times, patience,
love, sacrifices, and parenting
I willingly gave you

until you are developmentally ready,
when you are a parent yourself, maybe on your death bed.
I hope you can appreciate
the labor of love that quietly existed for you.

Maybe then you can forgive me
for any mistakes I made, as I grew up with you,
only having limited skills from my own childhood,
jealous people having demonizing those choices.

I want you to know that you *matter*,
and even though I didn't always know it,
so do I.

Thank you for being in my life.

HUMAN FACTOR

How do you come to sort out emotion?
Why is crying not okay?
When did it become a deficit
to be human?

There is strength
in functioning through tears
and being present
while being a whole person.

It is believed by some
that emotion's source is the soul
with no truer way to exist
than through its expression;

[95]

The path to Spirit
is by being in touch
with true
emotion;

Regardless of role, status, or perceived success,
you are a person first -
with hopes, dreams, fears and feelings
like any other.

When you can be all that is possible,
as a fully expressing human being,
regardless of societal labels,
have you not obtained the wealthiest status available?

Maybe that is why
we are asked
to separate out emotion and compassion
from what we must accomplish.

'UE-MA-'AH

Who is that image in the mirror?
A darker reflection
looking back at you,
with its own life and *will*;

Following you everywhere like a shadow;
A glimpse in the metal and glass or behind a tree;
Knowing your thoughts and deficits,
acting like a contrary force of nature;

Suffocating in dreams;
Tripping at the cliff;
Stealing everything so you will break.
An unraveling of life as you know it.

Too dangerous to speak its name
or even to write about.
Shhh! Don't call it over here!
You must overcome it when it comes to visit.

It will consume you,
if you do not love it to death.
You must embrace this enemy
to know it best.

RUNAWAY

Everyone said
don't run away from your problems;
Don't burn your bridges;

What a crazy thing
when a child feels
that they don't matter;

But life finds a way;
Children develop their own minds,
and others wait to snatch up the vulnerable,
to use them in order to meet adult needs;

Feeding lies to get what is desired,
using the young to go between
and bring back resources
for selfish purposes.

How do *Youth* know what is truth?
Battered and torn,
a rose dulled from abuse
now keeps dull for safety.

How much did you accomplish
by not listening to all of your Elders?
Rules were tough before you left.
Now life does not promote your well being.

What a realization it is in a garden of choices...
to learn that no one else really cares how you fare.
Once you have been used, you are tossed aside.

Remember who you were born to be,
which was to be all that you can be.
Return home to understand what you can;
Appreciate *boredom* and *restrictions.*

FORGET ME NOT

What is there to cherish at a memorial
when no one came by in life;
No celebrations along the way?

There are no pictures,
no laughter that haunts the halls;
Who was this person we called *relative*?

Do we steel ourselves from pain
or are we too busy for the complexities of relationship?
Were we too selfish to care?

What cost was there to talk?
...to do an unselfish deed
without being asked?

Even in the cruelest of homes,
can we not learn why this is so?
Is there no *silver lining* to explore?

Do we only come around
when there is benefit
to be had?

As children of the Old Ones,
we are not just victims of circumstance;
We are also Observers, Players and Voices.

With inner knowledge of the family,
can we not be strong enough
to react differently, object, speak out?

[99]

Is it possible to create a memory today?
Set the boundaries of the moment
and allow one joke to be told?

Cry not for the parted relative,
weep for wasted movements
and lost opportunities.

Recognize that the person you lost
was *you* from another generation,
your blood, your kin, your future.

So long as you are engaged,
even conflictually,
there is opportunity for kindness.

Like water against stone,
you may be the only hope
to wear away unhealthy walls.

Will it be said that you mattered
by making a difference and touching lives
or did you exist simply to express emptiness?

Will you only examine your part
when your time is done
and you are lonely or others come to take from you?

The connection you create now
creates the foundation for future generations
and eventually your own memorial.

What lessons do we leave our future
by how we engage or
abandon our role?

MATHEMATICS

In the way that the trees blow,
the tide comes in,
or the whales call,
...that is how my heart sings;

Like a Fibonacci pattern,
the cries of my soul
are the same at the source
as afar;

Calling to you
across the night sky
the stars shorten the distance
between our heavens;

I can still hear you breathe
as black matter fills my ears;
We are connected by molecules and stardust
so hear me call you;

Come talk to me in person,
don't stalk my dreams.
Memories of you reverberate in Dreamtime
until it is foggy whether you are just thinking of me,

or if this vision is just an echo in time,
forever and always,
repeating until I can't forget you,
into infinity.

KNOK-SEE-MEK'

Things that are terrible and ugly,
things that are unmentionable,
are left behind;

Thrown away,
no longer acknowledged;
Absence cutting down on the background noise;

Considered *"dead"*, *"disowned"*,
given a no-name:
"What's-His-Name", *"It"*, *"That One"*, *"Your* relative"....

Moved from the world of the living
to the world of exile,
a *not-worth-remembering-someone*
that crossed this way once.

There is power over being dismissive,
control rather than earnestly
moving on;

Romance attached to the pain of suffering,
by holding someone in limbo,
not affording opportunity for resolution,

because once that happens,
then One has to take responsibility for their part,
face the bitterness of mistakes,

the *enemy* becoming humanized,
and martyrdom ending;
Power and control dissipating.

There is no longer a *high* after surrender;
Divine Justice can take over
and truth can come about.

Deeds can be answered to with release to both captives.

Beyond the anger and the history,
there are still human beings involved,
with spiritual growth to occur.

KNOWLEDGE

Ever-needing,
my soul, ***dark-fired for beauty,***
hovers on the threshold of life,
thirsting for knowledge;

Like the willow branch that twists
and finds space never-ending,
thoughts grow forever
and through infinity;

With the passing of time,
dusk after dusk,
the weather of life wears away the wood
that once coursed strong with magic;

No longer are possibilities infinite;
Ideas are pruned back;
Magic and dreams withdrawn
as the season of youth passes;

The roots of my history
lie quiet beneath the green sodden earth,
clinging to moments past.
Waiting, waiting for more.

(Note - This poem was originally published in the Humboldt State
University's Young Writer's Conference Anthology dated April 23, 1983
through the Redwood Writing Project, Arcata, California:
www.RedwoodWP.org.)

HONEYMOON

Fair breathes the gentle wind,
blushing the bride and groom in the sight of the settling eve;
Silhouettes against the twilight,
hand in hand, walk into forever.

Frost begins to pluck at diamond studded stars
like an enchanting harp,
daring love to sing out,
though song has already tumbled from tender lips.

A silvered moon trembles softly,
dripping honeyed romance
while cool, electric sparks bolt atop the ocean waves,
laughing.

Two smiles pierce the night;
Hints of danger spin around
like little dust devils
along the moonlit beach;

Whispers are held back
as life seems to be pulled from human hearts -
captured by their own song written years ago,
just now being sewn into the universe.

A joining of spirits to an eternal journey,
a rejoicing of the depth of determination
that is tonight an awakening.

DEATH WISH

Stopped eating, no interest;
Pain has gutted your heart,
wishing to end it all.

Taking risks so you can die,
but that doesn't even work -
it'd be your luck that you'd only suffer more.

What's the purpose after all;
Everything you try, you fail at;
You are worthless.

You're not afraid, you don't care anymore;
You call for Death to come find you;
The Old Ways are gone,
there is nothing to stop what's happening to you.

Driving the car at 100 mph
so as to disappear in the wind,
become one with the cement.

It's too deep - genocide inherited for generations;
Drinking to cleanse the sorrow;
There is no quiet, just emptiness.

You cut or tattoo to wake yourself up;
You can't cry anymore - you're numb;
Who hears you? You don't even know what's wrong.

If only you had the words to acquire justice.
You wish you were Spirit,
but Death eludes you.

Dear Dad,

When I was a child, I was told terrible things about you. I witnessed how you acted. I believed what I was told. My development was not complete, I had no idea there could be more to the story. All I knew was that this was my reality. And you were our enemy. You were berated so much, I lost track of what I knew for myself and what was interpreted for me. I didn't know if it was Mom's story or mine. She was so psychologically fragile, that we all defended her/ the family, against you, the bully. We saw you drink, and beat us, then when you included us in your *affair*, it only confirmed what we *knew* about you. Us kids always had to be the adults. Mom was so afraid of being alone. She cried. She had no job. Even though we didn't know how to pump gas or change locks, we learned for her. The boys looking to you to model correct behavior, and hearing from Mom instructions on what it was to become a man. I was left to model Mom's behavior but you were absent to provide me instruction on being a woman. In order to survive, we had to bond with someone, so we chose the only available parent, even though she had never been parented herself. I became one of the instruments of her anger toward you. She taught me that *respect has to be earned* but neglected to say how. She showed us how to shut you out, cut you off, throw you away. Each of us not having a relationship with you because you left us with no choice but to take our mother's words for it. I was tasked to write you a letter *telling you off*. Afterward, I was welcomed into my mother's camp, but only for so long as it served her purpose, never my well being. While we tried to do something different for our own kids, Mom was still in the background and you were not. Our lives have all been built out of glass. You went on to enjoy your life, for your own self preservation, not taking responsibility for the destruction you contributed to. Because we were all enmeshed with our mother, we did not recognize

[107]

that she contributed too. Our pain was more than your absence and mistreatment, but also her pain. She still controlled how our lives reinforced hers, destroying all that threatened this. So afraid.

I stopped hating you somewhere along the way and didn't really think about you anymore. It was betrayal to talk about you. Everything was so black and white. I remember feeling unloved by you, justification for my beliefs. But degradation was the family value and then one day when Mom needed more support, she selected another scapegoat, someone else to be afraid of, so that the family would gather around her in crisis and keep her safe, the eternal victim, not once stepping up to take care of herself. Just like a child who never received the security that they needed as a baby, she made up stories and everyone believed her, some because they had always been jealous and could now become the family hero, some thinking they would benefit for money. No thought to destroyed lives. Only when she used the same words, the same comparisons, could I see that this was the same story she had told several times in her life. Professionals call it *parental alienation* and a cluster of behaviors including her not being able to individuate from her children or grandchildren, oppositional against everything that didn't feed her need. It had become her method of survival, blind to how it effected anyone else.

I apologize that I did not know any earlier. I wish that you had not abandoned us. I wish that there had been a way to talk about the pain we all suffered with at the time. If we had been able to understand why you hurt us, we would have found some answers. We felt unloved and you proved it to us by leaving. We needed a different life, not different parents. Now the family cycle is repeating. Who can stop it? It is part of our core now.

~I don't like you, but I think I've been coached to be biased.

[108]

FORGIVENESS

Hawk

watching the play of the field,
witness to astrological wheels of fate positioning;
A slow dance,
fully unseen by most;

Over-arching ideas
beyond understanding from rote or pen,
swirling cosmic patterns,
destiny unfolding;

Spiritual bodies jockeying for leverage
to brace against fulfillment;
Fortune not befalling the deserved,
but simply lying like haze everywhere;

The outcome unpredictable,
'save men who would
carve sieves for fortune
to trickle down hill;
Poverty to those without influence.

Yet stars sprinkle the path of all
regardless of accolades;
There is a price for every stolen bit of Heaven;
Each assumption,
a universal tab,
marking spiritual debts,
regardless of whatever label is attached;

Actions reflecting the inner universe;
Misinterpretations toll the heart;
Windswept by the invisible current of society,

the soul must brace to slow the impact
and shed the presentation of life
to receive Truth's great treasure.

Every action's origin and creation, a reaction;
So, cease blame;
Trust the unseen hands of Time;
Pull back the curtains of Heaven;
Look behind the door of this world
and comb through your dreams
to collect the pieces of broken furniture
stacked high,

...the props of Life's stage
needing assembly and care,
collecting thoughtless dust;
Choking the generations of characters
denied their script to face a critical audience;
Slow the cycle
to wish for self efficacy and happiness
in a clustered corner of time;

Seeking not sterility,
but freedom from poisonous congestion;
Life lived,
not set out like a place setting
and then damned for the arrangement;

To love the earthen carpet
set beneath our feet,
the foundation of forgiveness,
'else the root
to trip a life evolving;

So fragile the constructs
in an ever-changing universe
where survival has more value
than the fire of belonging to something greater than oneself;

Volatile constructs to diminish or embrace;
Our part should not be minimized
by tending to microscopic details
rather than relish in the delights
of the vast field laid before us;

We are so utterly fragile,
that we are too overwhelmed by the story of our lives,
even at times so very safe and happy,
to contemplate grace until it is lost forever;

Consumed.

PREDETERMINATION

"You will never amount to anything".
"You can never be a *Christian* because you are *Indian*".
"I know your type".
"I know your family".

"You are your horoscope".
"Your name has ill-fated numbers under numerology".
"You must pay for your father's sins".
"You are poor and not worth my time".

"You are a stupid...dirty...angry...wild *Indian*".
"Just because you're American, you are narcissistic".
"Just because you have *Indian* ancestry,
you are *Borderline* and *Depressed* as a baseline".
"I can tell by your picture what type of person you are".

How many turned up noses and angry faces
have to be confronted
to understand that we are marginalized,
dismissed, written off as *no good*.

Misinterpreted popular science psychobabble.

Kept down,
unable to get on our feet,
under the guise of politeness or fairness,
always knocked down.

Yet, for other cultures,
there is such a thing as growth, change, abundance.
Your diagnoses don't exist elsewhere
in the wide world.

Objectification, on the backs of the First People.

Break my spirit until I conform,
call the police before I get out of hand -
I'll agree to whatever name you give me
so long as you leave me alone.

HAPPINESS

Is it a family, a friend,
a milestone, a dream?
Is it wealth or comfort, peace or laughter?
Is it a prom, a wedding, a baby, a milestone,
a new toy, a routine, tradition, a house, a car?
Is it choosing to be a *fair weather friend*?
Is it diminishing others in order to feel better about yourself?

[112]

Could it still be a moment,
a glimpse of the sunset,
a letter in the mail,
an old photograph,
coffee?

Could it be privacy,
warmth, safety, cleanliness?
Perhaps appreciating others as points of light,
overlooking any shadow?

If you name it, will the jealous try to take it?
Could happiness come in a package
of unhappiness?

Do we see happiness only after we have nothing left?

Maybe it's the other side of the coin revealed in time?

LOVE LETTER

When once Love embraced me,
you pulled me close to your heart;
Our life strings wove together.

You captured my breath in yours
like the pale light of winter's sun,
illuminating a soul caught fire;

I was destined to be your counterpart;
Once two pieces of the same puzzle,
then only your other half;
Spiritually bonded together.

[113]

I knew you as myself,
able to *breathe-you-in* among a crowd,
understand your thoughts.

We moved as if life was a grand dance
no matter the distance in time or miles,
I belonged to you.

You bade me to "*dream, and dream of me,*
for in dreams there is truth,
and together we may find the truth
so let us dream as if we are one".

As with all dreams,
the waking hour came
and daylight separated us.

We were so young,
what did we know of life?
You went on to marry another.

Everything that I do from now on
will only be a shadow of what could have been.
My heart will belong to you forever, and always,

permeating the dimensions
of time and space
and dreams.

Love,
Me.

...IF YOU DISRESPECT ME, I'LL DISRESPECT YOU, THEN YOU'LL DISRESEPCT ME, AND I'LL DISRESPECT YOU, AND YOU'LL DISRESPECT ME, AND THEN I'LL DISRESPECT YOU....

SPIRIT SICKNESS

Have you tended to your responsibilities?
How about your yard, your relationships?
If your life is in chaos, look around.

You incur indebtedness by your actions,
non-actions;
Spiritual poverty for your crimes.

Grow to maturity
and connect your consciousness,
consider foresight management.

Don't meddle in things
you haven't earned respect for
if you don't want to get burned.

Justice is not yours to take
so watch what you do.
You have yourself to answer to.

Don't understand why things are happening to you?
Examine what path you are on.
Have you not been respectful?

Where are you supposed to be?
What is keeping you?
Whose ideas are you a prisoner to?

Sometimes we are born into sickness
with healing only possible
after living through it.

Balance will find its place
on this side
or the other side.

It will wait for you
until you want to get to it.

What awaits you
on the other side of the door
to this world?

Sometimes **fighting** is really about surviving

VANISHING

Nothingness is a pure state of mind...or...a genocidal tool.

It is not a difficult plane to reach,
stuck between worlds,
where the water has no ripples;

Where internalized oppression fills the void
and eliminates quantum
after a certain generation.

Is it good energy not to celebrate birthdays,
buy into holidays,
when deaths are no more than another day in passing?

Aren't we taught to
be invisible and keep our heads down,
work hard to overcome?

After awhile, nothingness means
not even a breath can be heard;
Humility becomes non-existence.

For answers,
go get right
with the World.

Put nothingness in your body
and let it awaken to reality
where meditation becomes realization.

Away from the processed, instantaneous world,
there is still wisdom
in not vanishing.

[119]

DIAMOND

Life
gifted to the most needy family,
deposited into the unseen cycling
of genocidal patterns,
corrupted communication
and deteriorating trust;
A melding of jealousy,
lack of tolerance and compassion,
where opportunities develop for evil to exist.

Emerges a lack of parental development, a stolen voice,
reshaped stories, ill-named visuals,
tentative relationships;
A young essence battered at every turn,
a near-extinguished spirit;
An unfulfilled life so someone else could shine.

Each experience, a cut toward evolution;
Only agates of love as rare gifts;
Beliefs forged through adversity.
Cast in darkness, dark-fired for beauty,
an internal flame ignites for justice.

Soul-infused brilliance shines through as destiny;
Truth revealed as the mantle erodes
in the cool of the atmosphere, absent all else -
abandonment, the last act of suffering;
The final calcination[6]; Setting of a gem.

---

[6] The 2008 version of *Re-poh Thresholds* used the word "crystallization",
however, upon reading Edinger's (1988) "*Anatomy of the Psyche*" the
more appropriate word was provided. Please refer to the *Recommended
Readings Index* for more information.

Demonstrating love can endure fire
and time uncovers equilibrium.
Rich when appreciated.
Fashioned to stand strong with clarity;

Alone, now outside of the eruptions;
Solid; Unable to become melded with others.

In overcoming the desire for retribution,
ends the cycle of violence through time,
outshining the bed of carbon;

Special because set aside as different.

PE-CHAN (BRIEFS)

Sincerity:
Running others off the road
in a hurry to get to Church,
interference in parenting;
Honor *whose* mother and father?
Minimizing life when it's *not your standard.*
But, hey, you're forgiven!
So, your way must be the right way?!?
You're so sincere, you must be telling *the truth.*

Anthropologists, Missionaries and Therapists for Hire:
With your mission statement in hand, fully funded,
do you understand that what you name
without background,
defines for people who they are,
without their ability
to do differently
and only reifies beliefs
about them?

One Version of Indian Love:
I might be nice,
but that restraining order
is *not* a love letter.

World Events:
Will RSS Feeds
save our lives?

Cupie Doll:
I wasn't born a doll.
I spent my life rejecting plastic,
until one day I wanted someone to play with,
so I changed my outside, which changed my inside,
and then I was discarded
because I wasn't worth the fight.

[122]

Polygraph:
YES or NO answers
and ways to debunk them,
where there should be explanations;
Why are they still used to measure
the vocabulary of someone
who doesn't speak those words?

My **HEADACHE** is not the same
as your headache.

Culture:
The only safe place for me
has been my culture -
and you think you *honor* me
by wanting to know about it?!?

O'-reen:
Capturing crashing wave,
day at the beach in a jar -
how you won my heart.

CRAZY is convenient.

What **MEANING** do you give that?

Balance:
What you give your energy to
becomes your focus.

Coyote:
Wannabe *Player*,
you threw away your family
to feed your ego....

ADD more words.

Social Worker:
Who are you to judge,
checking off legal boxes
for jurisdiction?

[123]

Follow the Dollar:
Why did this happen?
Who benefits from this act?
The answer is green.

Possibility Worker:
Advocate, teacher,
connection to resources;
No blaming or shame.

Father:
You are quiet strength;
Your childhood tucked away now,
did you forget life?

Tattoo:
Marked in culture, fun or pain;
Do not presume to know
or judge the point.

If you **TREAT** them
like they're crazy,
they'll rise to the occasion.

How:
It's not *black* or *white,*
yes or *no, this way* or *that,*
unless you just want to be *right.*
Think about how you want to express yourself
in order to get the answers you want -
there may not be another opportunity again.

Stolen:
Voice - so can't tell.
Success - to keep the status quo.
Chastity - to remove power.

Non-Truth:
If it considers
only one point of view,
it is inconsistent.

[124]

Algebra:
People are not problems,
equate them out!

Surprise ~ He's married!
Father of my child,
gun to the clinic,
my heart with a hole.

Massacre #18:
Like blood sprayed across the page,
at least my family is acknowledged.
Do you know why it lists
7 - 8 dead?

Remove the Dam:
Fish
are People,
too!

If you don't **TALK** with me,
chances are I won't understand.

Cats vs. Dogs:
No longer welcome in rentals;
Ordinances against *types;*
Now stats are out...on who is more *preferred.*

Vigilante:
In search of power,
seeking legitimacy
by hurting others.

Compatibility:
Mutant from your own culture,
sharing no one's worldview,
because you did something different;
Now of *Stand Alone* quality.

It's **OKAY** not to know.

[125]

Coaching:
First it starts slow,
redefining life's lessons,
coercion of words.

Depersonification:
Social media
promotes trading up people -
just *click* and *delete*.

Interfacing:
Everyone is fighting
their own personal battle.

What **PURPOSE** does DNA
collection serve?
And why is it done
without disclosure?

Kept:
If makeup makes you *feminine,*
then what are you when old age sets in,
but tossed aside
for the next painted face?

Dividing the Child:
Why don't children
have their own home?

Best Interests Standard:
The Indian Child Welfare Act

Whose needs are being met by creating
an **INVALIDATING ENVIORNMENT?**

When:
It's the 21st Century.
Will the United Nations ever agree
that Native American populations
are People?

[126]

Reflection:
You are yelling at me
for yelling at you
for yelling at me.

Where is your Frame of Reference?
How do you know disparity
unless you are told?

How will you know craziness
if you are immersed in it?

Cells:
Have we evolved so fast that
phones are killing
off our cells?

Threatened:
Don't get my adrenaline going
if you don't want me
to respond with adrenaline.

STICKS AND STONES may break my bones
and names can certainly box me,
but reframing can lead to deconstruction,
and seeing life on a continuum....

IF there are no pictures, are memories lost?

THOUGHTS are things.

Respect:
is not forcing
someone to fear you!

[127]

Bigger than...
How can you name or measure a thing
without first knowing
its place in the
Universal Continuum?!?

MISSION STATEMENT:
When did the business of the agency
become domain building
and legitimizing the individual
rather than helping the client,
using *self* as tool?

AT WHAT POINT do we stop crying
or being bitter and take responsibility
to end-cap those emotions and events
so we can grow forward?
Maybe when we aren't being hurt anymore?!?

Transparency:
Freedom is not about *no restrictions,*
but more about achieving the point
where One can see
through the complexities of life.

WHAT ARE THE THINGS
that you will do for
~~love~~   fear?

Non-traditional:
Making up culture
to copyright it;
Earning a degree
but abusing your clients;
Garbage and crime left behind for your profit.
What reputation do you leave me?
What will your relatives say?!?

[128]

Anger Dance:

Holding anger is protecting anger
and as a never-ending flow of
oppressing energy to its owner
(its focal point),
it simmers without justice
or resolution, reinforcing victimization
and revictimization.
Whispered as rumors and stories,
fed by the fire,
all encircle the creator
to protect a personal fear.

Mother:

Believing that your sons
won't live long
or are destined for
institutionalization,
you spoil them
...just a little bit more....

Indian Guide:

Trying to measure my *Indianness,* you tell me, "my friends
and I have been going up to *** (sacred site) on the
weekends. Have you ever heard of this place?!?" In
answering, "No, never heard of it; What's its *Indian* name?",
I am telling you that if it's not your place, it's someone else's.
You get a glint in your eye like you've won a battle of wits,
but the translation really is: "I'm not confirming where any
sacred site is, no matter who you tell that I'm not *Indian*
enough. And it won't be me who keeps you from wrong-
doing, the *Place* itself will correct you".

[129]

<u>Root:</u>
Pick up that thread!
It's your obligation.
Your right. Your duty.
Keep it alive and good.
It may have been lying there,
ignored all this time,
but you need to pick it up!
Every piece is valuable.
If not you ~ then who?
Disrespecting your roots
comes with a cost!

<u>STEPPING OFF:</u>
Coming off of soda,
step by step;
First no more sugar,
of any scientific kind;
Next goes caffeine and coloring,
reducing preservatives in my mind…

Until it's all gone – restoring health and controlling diabetes.

Wish we could come off of genocide,
layer by layer;
First removing stereotypes
(like we don't still exist);
How would it be if your comments
were reversed ~ you'd be pissed!

Don't forget to strip out invalidation:
massacres, suffering & unjust enrichment.
Real acknowledgement is due for our holocaust!

An apology counts for something
even if too much time has passed;
Peel away the layers that are lingering,

[130]

it's time to come clean…

Restore health and kill adversity.

How can we get this out of our system
and stop being eaten alive from the inside out,
without the parameters of acknowledgement for wrong?
Unless that has simply been the plan all along?!?

("In 2005, the American Psychological Association called
for the immediate retirement of all Native American
[Stereotypes] based upon their [detrimental] effect", apa.org)

One of my frequent dreamscapes has been the freedom of wandering through Victorian homes, arriving at each room through either a door, a window, or some other hidden nook much like the experience I had as a child when I visited my great grandmother's home and antique shop.

2 *Na' an'*

Teekw-tee-kwoh
(To Break Into Pieces)

RIGHTEOUSNESS

How foolish you are
with your authority and confidence -
lecturing, dictating, enforcing your version of the rules.

Have you ever examined language
to know what you speak of
does not exist?

You can name a thing with a word,
or label each part and piece
but in absolute truth....

a name is only a word
that has been assigned
to describe the relationship of the parts.

Our worlds are constructed
of beliefs about things
but there are always other ways of understanding.

Not all things are as they have been defined,
with labeling and projected personal bias applied
or naming in order to categorize importance,
for political reasons.

No word has the same meaning to every person
making our words a *trade language*[7],
only capable of defining relationships with context clues.

Dare not be righteous in your actions,
consider that there are infinite possibilities
and ask questions rather than dictate.

---

[7] As listed in the *Indexes* Section under *Recommended Readings*,
Getches, D.H., Wilkinson, & Williams (1998), cite *United States District
Court, Western District of Washington, 1974: United States v.
Washington: 384 F.Supp. 312.(W.D. Wash.1974). Affirmed 520 F.2d 676
(9th Cir.1975). cert. denied Washington v. United States, 423 U.S. 1086,
96 S.Ct.877, 47 L.Ed.2d 97 (1976)* as a prime example of trade language
truths. This case deals with a treaty wherein the Chinook Jargon was
used and understood to be two different things by the participants,
resulting in lawsuit.

TIERS OF REALITY

In our earnest conversations,
do we ever include
self-examination,
our
lens
to
the world?

The most tolerant of us
purport
there is
no *wrong* or *right*,
only conversation
that can bring us together
to create
reality.

We create context
with language,
through our relationships
and non-relationships;
Change the dynamics
by our very presence,
inaction,
action.

Yet, who are we
as professionals
to expect others
to honor
what it means to
embrace diversity,
appreciate *person-in-environment*,
if we can't do this ourselves?

[139]

Regardless of our
intentions,
worldview, background,
mastery of language and privilege,
can we ever be fully *present* with anyone
if we hold implicit beliefs
that some
should be
tokens
or targets?
Some can be dismissed as disabled?

Some will be
good
or
bad?

Do we generalize
patterns
and percentages
to fit our beliefs
or actually test the validity
of our daily thoughts
and processes?
Do we even see the tiers?
And from what angle?
How can anyone judge the depths
of another's thoughts
or tears?
And for what purpose?

Is there really *strengths perspective*
in idealizing,
being so helpful or too kind?
Aren't honoring and emphasis actually

exploitive,
absolutes?
Who are we
to define
what is more acceptable
than not?

And when we hold
unrealistic expectations,
or
tokenize
any person,
the reality is
the environment is set
for failure
because
we are all human,
living in tiers of reality,
ever-changing through time,
including all the unknowns we can't name,
and shouldn't give power to.

Does everything require a name?

When we are *present*
with anyone,
have we *joined* with their worldview,
understand the context of their reality
at that defining moment;
Or, is it really our perception
and previous experience
with their worldview?
Are we defining
the progress of any conversation
by our implicit, explicit, historic, idealistic,
privileged beliefs?

[141]

Who becomes
the favorite
or the target?

If we label our perception
of someone else's chaos
so that we don't lose ourselves,
do we not set the boundaries
of possibilities
that will ever occur?

If there truly is a way
to embody social work ethics,
then we would contribute to
an egalitarian society,
where there was
justice for all,
accepting differences
without judgment,
oppression,
or idealism;

Would we then be available,
to be *present*
for the rest of the world,
not to impose our own ideals
or create conflicts;
Not set others on a pedestal
and watch for them to fall,
to confirm that we were right
about them
all along?

SOOT-KOK'

See me for who I am,
not the degree I earned
or the job I do.

I am a person,
as human as you,
with joys and pains, much like you.

I am fallible.
I am vulnerable.
I am not a machine.

I see the world through
my experiences and pain,
sometimes with great beauty, sometimes not.

If I react to you
rather than respond,
you approach me in a disrespectful way.

I don't owe you any more confidentiality
then I would my best friend,
nor any more benefits than another.

I operate from a place of honor,
my family as my threshold of reputation,
not the rules and restrictions around me.

I apologize if I offend you,
but my truth is no less valid
than yours.

I may cry but that does not make me weak;
Beyond tears, I am cleansed,
and stronger for making a stand through it all.

Don't presume to know me,
you don't have a lifetime to walk my path;
Just acknowledge that I exist.

Because you label me or take things from me
does not take away from who I am.
I am whole and powerful in my own right to be.

SOCIAL ARCHITECT

YouTube redefining testimony;
Radio songs providing parenting skills;
Case law and popular belief constructing reality;
What is right and wrong belongs to who tells the tale;
Weighing truth against
motive and depth of comprehension;
Like witnessing a car accident,
to each his own,
unless you can convince those around you.

The power behind the words
and emotions behind those,
belong to the artist
who has pinned down
and captured the scene
in a word.

An audience falling in love
with the breath-taking,
somber, dramatic,
or brilliant story,
also captured.

Symbiotic dance;
Artist, story and audience
all sway together;
Each enjoying their private interpretation;
Later to breathe life into fantasy
and build upon incomplete ideas
as if they are fact,
evidence of life.

ACCOUNTIBILITY

Weeping from the well of my soul,
already imprisoned in my mind,
locked away since childhood -

trauma after trauma after reaction after reaction....
...finally...

embraced by walls and rules
until there is surrender
to being institutionalized,
an unrealistic dependency....

Why are people that are in need of *help* locked away?
How is there rehabilitation when prisons induct members
into gang and drug activity?
...And they come out "worse off" than when they went in?

What is happening when people who murder get less time
than people who struggle with addictions?
Are we just storing people,
or is there any real concern to change behavior?

If incarcerated people become institutionalized,
what becomes of the people locked in there with them?
Why did we establish a system of sentencing in the first
place?

Is it remorse that is sought? Is it pain that someone wants?
What about reimbursement for the crime?
Or an education so offenders learn something different?

What if every mistake carried the sentence of death?
Has it been forgotten that for every crime,
there is punishment beyond what humans can inflict?

Could punishment and correction become the same thing?
What if crimes were paid off
in dollars, compensation, reimbursement?
If it is such a great offense, why isn't the criminal indebted
to the victim...a slave?[8]

What is really accomplished?
A crime is occurring in reverse
when a true solution is not being considered.

So, what does it really mean to consider,
if the punishment fits the crime?

---

[8] Traditional Yurok law afforded victims of severe crimes the
opportunity to have their perpetrator pay off the balance of their debt
through a process not similar to America's "slavery".

D-V

Language is a gift
that excites us
and binds us together,
yet evaporates over time;

Words are a bridge
of symbolism
that mean different things
to different people;

Part of a skill-set inherited
on how to love,
grow, nurture
and evolve;

Interrupted with introduction
of behaviors
that take away the breath,
make the pulse race...

...a step beyond love
to feel so intoxicated,
so captured by another,
and in-tuned to one another's step;

Power enters the dynamic
when one tries to consume the other
painfully or suffocatingly,
maybe not noticed as dramatic at first;

Words begin to drop out of the picture,
the dance evolves;
At first romantic,
then moving to painful;

[147]

Before the dancing ends,
you are caught up again,
into the cycle,
believing romance can last forever;

Yet, the undercurrent,
the background music,
is void of the words
to heal and advance;

Violence spins out of control,
usurping every part of life,
unable to get things back
to the way they once were;

No escape from the embrace,
where would you go?
No one healthy speaks your language
any more.

OBJECTIFICATION

Unaware of your own biases,
to make matters easier,
you separate out concepts to help you
see the clearer picture;

Attaching names to things and people,
moving them into categories of
safe or not *safe*,
friend or *foe*;

A primitive brain function,
you see only black and white
while you move quickly
to discern your environment;

Later you can sort out
the truth,
to see if this label endures,
or if there are nuances;

With a name attached,
you then have a target
that you can
convey to others;

A "*common understanding*"
about a person or thing,
summed up in a name,
with the assignment of blame;

The greater the need –
those categories become more polarized:
those that *should* be exterminated,
those that *should* reproduce,
extremes to keep you safe.

By creating objects out of people,
they become *less than*,
marginalized,
without feeling or soul;

Objects are easier to put onto shelves,
or in concentration camps,
prisons, streets -
to outcast.

While no respect is paid
when it comes to *us versus them,*
those *others* are no less
human.

Otherization
insulating the popular group
and keeping away all else,
reinforcing confirmation biases.

Categorization that makes a part
seem larger than life
when it is not the whole story,
nor the most important.

Depersonification
as a window, an opportunity,
the root cause of intention for harm;
Evil.

WHAT'S IN A LIE?

Is it *what is said,* or *not said,* or *who benefits?*

If you track the original statement
and see if it changes over time,
can you see the inconsistencies?

When one talks highly or poorly
about a matter,
you should know that there is personal attachment;

If the speaker cannot practice
what is preached,
why are the words being spoken?

[150]

Who benefits from words
being different from actions,
or non-actions?

If there is a change in the story
or avoidance about a topic,
what is the resistance?

There does not have to be
intent to deceive or harm caused for it to be a lie;
It could just be habit or lack of language skill.

It may be all but a matter of convenience,
a crime of opportunity,
the damage to victims considered low.

So how to catch a lie?
Go to the source.
Collect every piece of the story without distortion.

Research a non-vested source,
trace the inconsistencies,
and think for yourself.

NO SUCH THING AS MONEY

What if wealth were measured by honor,
hard work or being blessed by a Divine Source?
What value would that carry?

How did it come to be that dollar bills
or chunks of nickel, copper or gold
meant wealth and those without, its slaves?

The term *money* is generic for an exchange
of one thing to get another
but what is looks like has changed over time.

Money as a social construct,
is made believable by those who participate,
yet not the only method.

What would the American world be without it?
Would we cease to exist or starve
or would only businesses who exist on this construct
crumble?

The magnificent dollar has been worshipped so long
that sacrifice for it has been land, entitlements,
species, natural resources, life, relationships.

If there was no such thing as money,
and only the belief in the relationship that money serves,
what would it look like to do something else?

CONTINUITY

What chain are we pulled by?
What current sweeps us away?
What rope do we hold to
in order to survive?

To bridge our gap of understanding
from the generations before us,
we must make sense of our world;
Continuity for empowerment.

Caught up in the vision or illusion
of our ancestors,
will we ever question the interpretation
of reality set out for us?

If our identity is supported by the links of generations,
the worldview of an entire set of people,
how can we disconnect from continuity
without losing everything?

Our thoughts about role, authority, life...
parenting, consequences, respect...
are all the responsibility of our ancestors.
When and how do they become ours?

We capture a moment by labeling it,
but life is fluid and ever-changing
and can only be bridged for a time;
There is no such thing as ownership.

We can not possibly have the maturity
to comprehend all,
so we rely on our Elders and their experiences
and grow from that place.

Should there be a kink in the rope,
introduction of genocide,
an Elder whose needs surpass those of the new generation,
payment of deeds done will be passed along.

And how would we know it
if genocide was passed along?
...Because of the measure of relationships
or quality of life around us?

[153]

It may become the mantra *not to dwell on the past*,
but all must be made right,
worlds reopened, language changed;
Patterns will continue if healing is ignored.

Justifying or ignoring inappropriate actions
severs continuity and complicates the lifeline.
See beyond the turbulence
and let life flow undammed.

Re-evaluate the personal myths to understand the source.

PUE-NO-MEEHL

Personalizing every event,
believing that *fault* should be assigned,
it's *all or nothing*;

You chalk it up to *bad character*.
Not able to think things through,
and see that you erred
in perspective, language or thought;

You are the mad scientist who *creates a monster*.

You focus on a *critical* factor
and distort it to mean *everything*,
sucking the goodness from the larger picture.

Just because you *want* to believe it
doesn't mean it will be true or permanent.
There will always be more to the story;
It is your choice to acknowledge this;

Before you punish or demonize,
you should slow down for the whole story;
Stop *labeling* which causes anger,
recognize how you *contribute.*

If you walked in those moccasins,
would you see yourself as labeled and be angry,
or feel like you're being told what to do
and *rebel?*

Did you create a *hopeless situation*
so the *monster* fights to defend its life?
Do you *examine* your hurt feelings
and find a real cause or just your emotion?

Should you *focus* on problems
and *minimize* the positive,
life will consume *your behavior*
and thoughts.

Everyone around you
will appear to be *out to get you* -
So you will have to label some more,
tell others what they should do;

Trigger the monsters
so they *respond* to you more severely,
so you can create more chaos
and dig yourself deeper into your *martyr* box.

Rather than lose
more opportunities
for happiness,
could you see things *differently?*

Are people really changing their normal way
and acting so differently than ever before?
Is their behavior *not warranted* for the situation?
Or is that what you want to believe?

Maybe they can't name it themselves,
but there is usually a *pea under the mattress*,
a root cause, a medical condition,
an *environmental trigger* building up.

Things do not *magically* happen;
If there is no word, there is at least a definition.
You must take *responsibility* for your part in the choices
and your ***distortions...***

before you make *yourself* a monster.

REAL INDIAN

He's not a real *Indian* -
He's got a job, drives a car,
and wears store-bought clothes;

She's not a real *Indian* -
She's never been to the Reservation,
can't speak the language and doesn't want to;

They're not a real *Indians* -
they don't get casino money,
they cut their hair and go to Church;

What defines *Indian*?
Is it the government who wants
their government-ward responsibility gone for cheap?

[156]

Maybe it is survival instinct to marry pale
and move away from the rez
or the adaptability gene that affords a modern mind?

We inherit 100% of each parent's blood,
making us 100% real;
A full blood to the Human Race.

Indians are human
be they traditional, urban, suburban, rural, frontier, rez.
So who can say they're *Indian*?

Legally, ethnically, culturally, racially, tribal
are all recognized American *Indians*.
Some are only a few due to genocide or politics.

Mostly, there has had to be sacrifice
to win their place on a lucky list,
the same list modeled for Hitler's genocide.

Do we have to be romanticized
with beautiful Abs
or a sense of humor to matter?

Indian Way is to bring others along,
exclusivity eliminates strength.
Let us not sort through who is more *real*.

It shouldn't be a story about privilege and power
~ or we will vanish.

TRUTH DANCE

When reality is misnamed for you
and you wander the streets
with the breeze on your frostbitten face
looking for sustenance,

truth molded
like plated gold or frosting on a cake,
around what it would look like in a lawsuit,
your soul aches for understanding.

Constantly fighting the blackness
enveloping you,
stories that could be, should have been,
might be made to be;

Pick a truth, any truth,
and stick to it,
follow it through;
Your life depends on it.

What is real and what is imagined?
Who is behind what things mean?
You remain in a womb, undeveloped as a person,
constantly enduring turmoil.

It feels like you were never meant to be born.
When can you have your life returned to you?
Sometimes things are right, sometimes wrong
because the story continues to dance around you;

Until you get angry
and can pin the truth down,
or get dangerous
so that truth holds still.

[158]

Long enough for you to see
the mess you have caused
because you followed
someone else's truth,

even if you did not know
any other truth
because your world
was painted by your creator.

When Fear leaves you
and the warmth of Life fills you,
you will know
the inconsistencies.

You can then master your world,
identify the shape shifters
and story tellers;
Magicians who do you no justice.

The thread of truth to follow
is to understand who benefits from the story,
where does the money flow,
what is left out of the story that you can not see?

You might fight to find the right words to use
and not continue the legacy of lies,
not truly meant for deceit,
but handed down as the story needing to be told;

The stronger you become,
you will find that enemies will come forward
to protect their constructed fantasy,
and take power from your strength.

[159]

Do not let jealousy overcome you,
or be guilted or shamed.
You have a right *to be* -
your world just as valid as anyone else's.

No matter what words they use,
the truth can not be denied,
just as the dark
can never diminish the light.

As the Champion of your world,
others may not trust you,
and try to tear you down,
but they can not move you from
the respect granted each Life.

HEARTBREAK vs. HEARTBREAK

Crow came by to tell me...

Something wasn't right at your house. Now I can see you have a black eye, what has happened? Why does your family continue to fight each other? Will this only stop when someone dies or an outside agency sets the parameters for you? You seem to lack internal equilibrium.

Your story is the same as your mother's and your daughter's, a pattern repeating in the generations. What you get, you find as normal and pass along. No one's heartbreak is more devastating than the other's. Once you teach abuse, your family becomes familiar with it and invites it in. A lack of social skills and intimate bonding are missing, so everyone seeks it out and is unsuccessful. The family is angry and overwhelmed, looking for blame. Manipulation has become a means for self preservation. Do you love your family enough to do something different?

Crow said he looked in a reflective pool and saw where your family repeats its mistakes. You have to be quick to see it too. Look for the exceptions, to see where self-preservation exists. Who has done something different? Where can something different happen? Look to the people who have been excluded from the family, they hold answers, repeating and folding back on to each other, through time and historic memory.

Crow says you need to break up the behavior and let it go in the wind. He showed me that your family needs a mirror so everyone can talk about what's going on.

[161]

STEREOTYPE SOUND BITES

City, urban, country, rez...
like a fast burning candle,
life is on *Indian time* -
no matter how hard you try
it happens when it's meant to be.

Rep-chem is one name for the monster
who stalks the Sweet People,
attracted to the smell of stress,
soda, alcohol, meth.

Token Spokesperson worn by *Indian* years,
you are the Mystical Mascot,
contrary to popular culture,
not quite able to interface with society -
How does your casino grow?

The Visitors want you to
give them an *Indian* name,
bless their crystals and sing a song;
Are you hungry enough yet
to be their dog-and-pony-show?

Fry bread was born out of rations;
Potlatch jokes born out of necessity -
Elders eat first;
No, its age before beauty.
Don't forget to laugh at yourself, Coyote.

Women are Life Bearers.
Those who can't bleed find a way.
We learned quickly,
men would be killed but women only hurt,
so women have become Culture Keepers.

[162]

What place for men?

When *Bluecoats* took *Indian* brides
to access their trusts, for land,
tradition was inherited
from woman to woman
and Life still happened.

It's not safe to be *Indian*.
Statistics show it's a risk.
White is right,
except for matters
of historic knowledge of what works best *naturally*.

Indians were conquered a long time ago,
so why don't they go back to where they came from?
Never mind that Title wasn't extinguished
and treaties were used to stave off wars
the government couldn't afford.
The federal apology is never coming,
atrocities unanswered;

Our worse enemy, ourselves,
until we can talk about
the institutional sound bites.

(Note - This poem is made up of commonly heard stereotypes and
publishing of them does not imply that there is any truth or correctness
to the words. They have been put to print in order to eradicate them,
remove any negative power, have speakers examine what they say even
in jest.)

CONFIRMATION BIAS

Your words of comfort are
shaming, blaming, labeling.
You define for me what I should believe.

You don't know me
or what things mean to me.
You didn't care enough to ask.

You projected your world on mine
and insulted me,
devalued my feelings and thoughts.

You assume too much, being ego-centric,
a crusader, a colonist, a missionary, a savior.
We're not speaking the same language.

My advice to you
is to examine your own advice.
God did not make you *better.*

How do you benefit from harming me?
Do you collect some power?
Or excuse some wrong you committed?

What happened to
starting from a place of *not knowing,*
a person as knowing their *own* life?
Are you so privileged you can't see your own arrogance?

Do you remember what it is
to *do no harm*?
Do you intend to give good guidance?

[164]

When you disrespect me,
you are asking me to take your hand-me-downs
and I recognize the power dynamic,
so I am no longer open to you;
No matter what I say or do,
you already know the outcome.

Maybe you're just pornographic,
excited at my perceived drama
or your perceived ability to influence titillating details.

I am not your trophy, your conquest or your thesis statement,
and the world does not evolve around you.
In fact, you have only shown your true colors.

MY TRUTH

Once, I spoke when I was not wise.
I wanted to contribute what I knew.
I was full of life.

When telling anything less than the whole truth
is considered an insult against the Creator,
how would I know to monitor my level of disclosure?

I did not think to include every perspective.
I did not include a disclaimer or list any exceptions.
Should I have remained mute until I was old?

American language doesn't respect advance apologies;
Wasn't it implied that I do not have all the answers?
Why didn't *you* contribute to the conversation?

Even people in positions of power
make mistakes and speak from one dimension.
Does the listener judge based upon the speaker's
development?

Moreover, what's to guarantee we speak the same language
even when we use the same words?
Don't they hold different meanings for each of us?

If we're only ever speaking a trade language
and learning more from interpersonal expression,
in what situations will we know we are on the same page?

How does any word or speaker have credibility?
When will we know a word is filtered through personal bias?
Where is the wisdom?

People don't have long enough life spans
to earn answers for themselves
and no one listens to Elders anymore.

From now on, I will *ask* not *tell*.
I know that I will never know everything,
therefore, I will speak of nothingness.

Unless it is speaking to my truth.

CIVILIZATION

Compost pile
growing at the foot of the car,
no time to eat at home;

Migrating to the grocery store
in *Warrior Packs*,
protecting the family purchases;

Communing with nature
from the soft, safe
protection of the couch -n- T.V.;

Love and relationship
developed, expressed, and dissolved
over cell towers and internet lines;

Beauty measured by plastic, paint, money,
no natural selection
or clean DNA;

Everything is about the dollar
so the incentive is greed,
not honesty or grace;

Gaining weight
because gravity is disappearing
or the processed food doesn't digest; BPA's;

Housing
is poisonous indoors and out,
if you didn't take out a loan and lose yours;

Gangs roll down the street,
identifying themselves as those lost
through the cracks of civilization;

Happiness is sought
through who has the most toys,
not spirituality or connectedness;

The foundation of society
is based on paper construct,
words, laws, definitions and politics.

The North Pole
is vanishing.
Santa Claus has had to relocate;

T.V., car, dishwasher, washer/dryer,
air conditioning, radio, heater, oven, phone,
electricity, plumbing...

Does anyone remember how to do without?

What will happen when these things
do not exist
that we put into place?

No water for crops or bathing or drinking...
remove one basic element
and what happens to civilization?

We have forgotten
how to even talk to each other absent *things.*
Do we remember where things come from?

Are humans so omnipotent
they can glue society together
through all these constructs?

WHAT'S REAL

Words, money, possessions, time
are all fragile constructs,
contingent upon things that are real,

which are said to be the spaces in time
where reality is created,
between two people in conversation;

And the relationship between objects
that creates a certain function
for a particular response,

the fresh air,
rushing water, living Earth and
breathing creatures;

There are many realities
than can be true
at the same time.

Black and White categories
are reinforced to keep others from knowing
there is a world of multi-faceted colors,
all viable and important.

Without relationship,
no creation would exist as we know it;
Would we then just be spirit?

[169]

So why do we consume so much reality
in order to prop up social construct
that reality suffers and fades?

Why have we eliminated diversity
and inflated or deflated labels
in order to pretend the status quo is reality?

CHPUER-KOK'

Passivity is seen in America
as weakness, vulnerability,
something to attack, exploit or remove.

Yet saplings survive the storms
and water wears at rock;
Shouldn't gentleness be valued?

Don't underestimate the strength of silence;
A leader can not lead without followers;
Diversity of voice ensures survival.

Rigidity of thought and word,
allows passivity to leak through
and thrive in hostile environments.

If everything is conquered
by physical destruction or constructing terminology,
Life moves away

...but finds a means to sprout through the cement,
rise above entrapment.

Where assertiveness disappears,
passivity takes over,
ever-present.

Because I exist,
I hold sway.
I am strength.

FORENSIC EVALUATOR

You assess with your clinical mind
and fit things into categories
ruling out mimics and exceptions;

But do you consider
that only biological illnesses can be pigeonholed
or that some things are written on sloppy statistical tests?

The original knowledge doesn't belong to you
yet you cite it and say you understand it
and you take things personally, even leaping with it.

Do you also look at what is missing?
Where is the shadow of an object?
What is withheld, untold or unnamed?

Your worldview teaches you to see things narrowly,
straight-ahead, the outliers ignored.
The truth is that there are many possibilities influenced by
many factors.

What if someone has a different learning style
...is processing so much information due to
sorting out second languages or...

[171]

having clarity beyond your limited words?
Do you see the current story
or the story that passes
through one generation to the next?

Do you remember saying words that are dualities
or only have *yes* or *no* replies?
Did your word mean the same thing to me?

When you can't comprehend a thing,
do you scorch the earth trying to destroy it
or are you above working with other ideas?

...maybe it is all about validating your position
because you can't be wrong,
defending the status quo,
or supporting your livelihood off the misery of others?

When was the last time
you renewed
your license requirements?!?

MULTIPLICITY

I see the world differently than you,
because I am not you,
not because I'm crazy.

You should understand this,
as the American Way is founded
on the principle of mutiny to escape tyranny.

My way is the Way of the Earth.
I walk it, I talk it,
I have to alter my thinking to communicate with you.

[172]

You build your world on social construct -
what it means to be popular or rich;
Some even forget about "*wealth in Heaven*".

I build my world on Spirit,
what is right with the way I honor others,
as there is no true prosperity to hurting another
just to gain some.

There is no such thing as
a path to happiness,
Happiness just is.

For over 500 years,
People have tried to silence our voice
but we have not gone away.

Lately, we have not had to speak -
Earth speaks for itself.
Now what will Your Way mean?

My Way means sometimes I walk in pain;
It is the sacrificial pain of doing right.
It is my duty to consider all others.

I also know that if I do not honor My Way,
which is what you call *tithing*,
it comes out of my hide later.

There are many ways of being in this world
just as there are many ways to any destination,
and all can be valid at the same time.

Variety is the essence of survival,
an *in-between* on the continuum of extremes;
There can be more than two valid thoughts.

It makes for a complicated world
to consider all possibilities,
but what a wondrous depth of life!

So when my language doesn't make sense
and I don't think linearly,
that doesn't make me immature or ignorant.

I am a multi-dimensional thinker,
simultaneously considering this world and others;
I am trying not to be offended by your thinking.

When I was less mature,
I did not even realize you lived in a different world,
next to mine.
I interfaced with your world in a raw and violent way.

Now that I am wiser,
I can ignore my embarrassment to ask you
what you mean by your insults, words and actions.

Even when I can consider the *both/and* possibilities,
I may or may not attempt to raise you up,
and I don't have to be your teacher or *Indian* Guide.

I have enough heart to contain it all.

A NEW WORD

People are not rainbows,
or fruit,
or shades of color;

Color is a legal construct
created before the last century
by which to sort people;

White, Black, Red or Yellow,
the mythical and categorized,
became legal measurements; Institutionalized;

Unsupported by evidence,
the labels stuck,
determining land owner, slave or servant.

History shows that despite assigned status,
some didn't play by the rules and survived,
some suffered through and still survived.

Without judgment of who is stronger,
who is smarter or more privileged,
we need a new word.

We could consider caring for the vulnerable,
guiding the underprivileged,
become more of a collective;

Harvesting every talent,
encouraging every difference,
welcoming the richness of strength at every turn.

The contrary would be sterile -
cornering all into
a *potato blight starvation.*

Therefore, perspective is necessary
as a Nation,
a *melted pot* of Peoples,

making mistakes and having successes
based on their resources and upbringing,
not shade.

Some have even altered their perception
or language or culture
to tolerate how they have to exist.

This has less to do with color
than history
and it is time to see people as they are:

People are simply Human.

Unless your objective is to hold *Power Over.*

TURN OF A WORD

Listen!
Did you catch it?

Shall, should; Will, would; Discuss, argue;
Be, become; Racism, exploitation; Know, believe, think;
Munchausen's Disease, Parental Alienation;
ADHD, hyperactivity, hypervigilent;
Active efforts, culturally and socially appropriate;
House, home;

One word can change the intention.

Did you get mad because you thought
you were told what to do,
when you were only offered the suggestion?

You ran with what you heard
and didn't look back,
making leaps about what was said.

Suggestion, recommendation, directive,
implying, commenting, observing,
demanding, telling....

If you had stopped to hear,
you may not have paired your biases and predictions
with what was said and been offended.

Why didn't you ask for words,
to clarify the picture
before you jumped to the defense?

Are you unaware that you are trapped in your situation?

Could you be so arrogant that the Speaker
did not approach you in the right way,
or talk your language?

Were you watching for physical cues
that didn't make sense to you?
Since communication is culturally bound and mostly visual,
you missed out.

So guarded are you that you believe the worse!

Step back and examine why you are so quick...
what pain do you carry that you create chaos
by your response? by your reaction?

CO-OPTED

Academic teacher,
worshiped by many,
your idealistic words drip of calm inspiration,
romanticizing other cultures.

Your dream to create a paradigm shift,
to be more inclusive,
only goes so far
as it means prestige.

Infecting others with this thought,
you are inhibited by wanting a job;
Picking and choosing that which you will defend
in the plight of whichever *minority*.

Blaming and shaming,
you ignore your part in the process.

[178]

What you seek to change is only perpetrated
in order to maintain comfort and familiarity.
In fact, you are just human,
blind by language
and worldview;

Placed on a pedestal,
you were destined to fall from grace,
your disciples to carry on the same after you.

OLD MAN JUSTICE

Old Man Justice,
you are the foundation
of our society.

Thank you for being available
for us to bring
forward our concerns.

Without your forum,
there would be no avenue
so we could be heard;

Truth would not be known;
Those in power would
continue to oppress us;

People with damaged souls,
attempting to hurt us
for their own gain;

You are our safety net
so we don't bleed
or flounder in poverty;

[179]

Our hope
so we don't take justice
into our own hands.

EEOC, Union, Labor Commissioner,
Complaint Division, Department of Ed,
Supervisor Board,

our medium for validating
us as human beings,
not servants to a cruel ruling class.

Until the veil is lifted
and it becomes clear
that a facade is no longer needed.

Who funds your activities
that you can choose
which cases to consider?

Has it become that society is
so trapped by the rules that govern
that there is no longer reason to pretend?

As the working public,
we are slaves to having a job
and answering to an employer;

We have no choice when you choose
not to follow your own regulations;
Who can afford to file a lawsuit?

What will we do when you choose
not to interview witnesses
or send us our own documents?

...Can't schedule the weighing of evidence;
Watering down testimonies?!
Where then is Equity?

Long gone and buried?
Thank you then for allowing us
to weep at her gravesite.

At least we
were given a place
to be heard.

TOO'-MO-NEEHL

Over the mountain they came,
looking for treasure beneath the earth,
exploiting land, people, each other;

Inserting genocide,
removing what could be taken,
spoiling what could not.

Waves of destruction came
in many forms,
personally, professionally, systematic, policy;

Years of battering,
undermined healing,
moving genocide into worldview.

Traditional methods of life corroding;
Violence, language,
much tainted by the aftermath;

Where women were once treasures,
bride prices paid to families
in order to marry daughters,
then there were daughters with dowries,
in order to have value enough for marriage,
to husbands who objectified them;

Where once the family fought
to preserve goodness
and keep away enemies,
Families then learned
to fight
and sacrifice each other;

Creating internal-chaos
in order to band together
and fight a common enemy.

When people are thrown away like garbage,
rather than being helped or recycled,
or tainted and reintroduced to infect a population,
genocide does its job.

ONENESS

How easy it is to lazily identify with the world
in which we are immersed.

Happily attaching labels, colors, meanings
to all around us.

Should we reduce our understanding
to its basic form and element,
could we see that everything is related...
perhaps stardust, expressed in different patterns?

[182]

What if we stopped sorting things into categories,
and joined our emotions with the basic map of life?
Could we not become One with the universe
...filling hunger with all of our senses?

Like our bodies, absent preservatives,
finding balance with the environment;
Nutrition breaking down to basics for assimilation,
speaking a similar language with cells for optimum oneness;

Energy converting
from one form to another;
Existence on a singular level, together.

Once we can comprehend this miracle
that we are all interconnected,
able to communicate
with the same molecular understanding,
would we not have the ability
to reach out in ways we have forgotten possible...
extending ourselves by immediately joining
with other extensions of Life...

elements connecting at their simplest form,
singing the same song in the same tone,
able to reach out and become part of our Relations,
freed from our boundaries...

... permeating the windshield that protects us...

...that then touches the air around us,
and is a part of the plants and trees and animals...
which are also a part of us,
and everything else...

...Surrounding, immersed,
saturating all of us,
each part of the other...

Communicating with our hearts
dreaming the same dreams,
speaking without words...

If we remove visual and social construct,
does our world not become a basic pattern;
Is it not possible to achieve oneness
by removing the definitions that bind us?

(While this poem reflects a Native concept of interconnectedness,
quantum physics has also been empirically exploring similar ideas. One
such experiment is *Erwin Schrodinger's Cat*, which has led to further
discussions about alternative realities.)

FLOWER DANCE

Mother wants Daughter to have good character.
Prepares for years ahead.
Mother's regalia.

When it is time for Daughter to enter the Spirit World
and find her own medicine,
become strong to live a good life,

Mother gives Daughter to Gram
for ten days,
knowing that she has taught all that she can.

Mother takes a position outside of the immediate circle
to allow Gram and Role Models to teach,
supporting those who support her family.

Everything in prayer and tradition,
honoring of relatives in Spirit World,
honoring of relatives in this world.

Children call to the girl to come back to childhood;
Father guards the way;
Daughter makes her own way to womanhood,
demonstrating character.

Conducting herself as a strong and capable being,
she is introduced to the larger community
and respected as a treasure,
only as strong as she was supported.

Emerging from the Spirit World,
everyone wants to be a part of the good luck;
New strength in the community.

[185]

One of the first ceremonies
to be removed
when the Settlers came.

UNBALANCED POWER

Unconscionable for you not to exist,
Power Monger attracting bees to honey,
like stench on rotting meat,
seeking customers for job stability:

Oversight agencies know the system is broken
with the answer found
by following the dollar.
Who do you answer to?

Internal investigations result in sound bites
of some who will be hired
or policy altered
but nothing really changes.

If there aren't enough trained workers,
federal waivers can be acquired
to hire uneducated people and save money,
resulting in preserving the cheaper employee

and maintaining an agency culture
where you can't be a wallflower
nor stand out -
you must know the *right* people.

Indentured students can be recruited
straight from universities
and must endure hazing or never work in the field again
in the name of preserving the culture;

[186]

All the truths are the foundation
for perpetuating the cycle
and preserving the layers of incest
that are familiar in most institutions.

Documents can be altered or disappear
as *an issue of training* or *a work in progress*
without permission or oversight,
sometimes fraud, construction of events or politics.

Embedded in the cubical walls
are the whisperings and social networkings
that change families' lives for generations,
depending on the clique or stability of the source.

Sometimes fate has to do with the political agenda,
the emotional state, or the time afforded the supervisor,
rather than the reality, importance, or human component
of any given situation.

A power trip of definitions,
a construction that fits the need;
What layman can speak this language
when there's a bounty on the heads of children?

Judges, Lawyers, Others respect their words,
not having time to question the legitimacy,
but employees are all overwhelmed
at times slapping things together to keep from liability.

Ethical or not, workers are subject to corruption,
not trained, misinformed, biased;
Afraid of losing their job, or becoming a client;
Co-opted.

Subject to their environment,
they are not necessarily evil,
but surviving in a jungle
long overgrown and wild with power.

The toxic office is a systematic problem
with the face of good intentions,
not unlike other institutions,
that suck money, foster corruption and feed the top.

Lost in the political structure
are the children
whose safest placement is not in stranger care,
or the overwhelmed parents
whose culture doesn't interface well.

DOMINATE

Does power and control have to look like:
those who take the resources rather than share with others,
the privileged protecting what they have,
others fighting to gain control?

Rather than seeking to make another *less than,*
and checking off the box in order to hold jurisdiction,
whether it's believed to be for their own good or not,
denying grace so someone else benefits,

why not use the same criteria of *naming*
to have another type of conversation
about moving beyond limits and toward something
different?

Instead of boxes, seeing life on a continuum?
With words, anything can be created;
Poison can be removed from the supply;

Power Over
can become *shared power.*

Putting unlike pieces together,
bound to the same fate,
in harmony;
Learning to speak a common language
and weaving in a similar thread
instead of being divisive;

The solution lies in back-weaving,
becoming more inclusive,
nothing being wasted,
for a stronger whole.

Diversity uniting;
Community needs being met
so no one brings another down;
No poverty or abuse to those without.

By shaping the work, relationships become watertight;
Fibers of an original destiny, now intertwined,
each piece a valued part for a common benefit;
Progress not possible without the environment supporting
the effort.

Upon completion, a thing of beauty and practicality.

My Grandmother often said that she kept her relationships with the people of her past in the waiting rooms of her mind until she was ready to deal with them.

3 *Nahk-se-mee*

Pkwe-ko-mey-ye-tek'
(To Bring Out Treasures)

RELATIONS

Relations...

created by cosmic design, embedded in time,
with the sole purpose of divine expression
as it relates to everything else;

Winter to Spring
to Summer and Fall,
all creatures responding to
Flora and Fauna;

Mountain jutting upward;
Slide leveling growth;
Ocean wearing away Earth;
A cycle of creation;

Kissed by weather
and embraced by light,
what are human souls
but further triumphs of life?

A Spirit World existing
concurrently
and in relation
to the one we are awake to;

Spectrums of expressions,
some found in the light,
others fired in the dark,
what is seen and unseen;

From birth to death, life blossoms
from natal bud to dying petals curling inward;
Everything is related.

[195]

VEIN

Life's sweet blood trickles
over rocks and moss
on its journey homeward;

Gathering minerals on its way,
bitter and sweet alike,
composing true colors;

An endless circle of decisions,
only its Heavy Song knows the way,
beating a path homeward;

Only a merry heart could be so wise
so sure of pulse and inward eyes,
finally home, where strength is pure and fear is dead.

INTERNAL CLOCK

Breathe in, Breathe out.
Only mindful of breathing.

Like Ocean teaches...
in and out...

Breathing while swimming,
breathing under stress, breathing for joy...

Cleanse yourself of pollution,
strength in, poison out....

Water doesn't complain about any dirt,
and still comes in... and out...

Breathing as a young person,
in middle age or as an Elder...

The form may change,
but the spirit is the same.

Breathe in, Breathe out.
Pace yourself to embrace life.

Breathing is the pendulum
of your journey on Earth.

[197]

MEMORIES OF HEKW-SA'

Elusive *Hekw-sa'*,
seen at a distance as a mist of air,
and close, surfacing next to boats as a gentle giant;

Baby *Hekw-sa'*, curious about Beach Combers,
swimming right up to the drop-off at the surf,
wanting to play with others.

Momma calling Baby back to the pod,
Baby turns reluctantly,
Humans left sad in the surf;

Hekw-sa' popping out of the Ocean in concert,
or to catch an *Eagle's eye view*,
joyful for the sunbeams hitting the water;

Their haunting song, like echoes in dreams,
a family unit protective and loving,
grazing the sea.

Why would their life's journey
be less valuable than ours?
Any less beautiful or tragic?

Now simply sport for sonar.

(Note - 10/2008 United States Supreme Court issued a ruling not to alter
military sonar tests due to *lack of evidence* that testing effects whales and
dolphins)

[198]

DANDELION PUFF

When I was but a *thought,*
I had one wish - - - to grow up.
As I blossomed,
I developed into this thought.

Battered in the wind and hail,
cool youth-hood of pain,
no sweet warm sun for me,
none, save that reflected by the Moon.

Then I had a wish.
I dreamed it full bloom.
It is my wish come true.
In this other thought...

I, myself, am a wish,
therefore, I can want.
Peace might be my destiny
if it was my only thought.

When from nowhere came a boy
who had but one wish
and I was his thought.
How sad it is to be just a wish.

(Note - This poem was originally published in the Humboldt State
University's Young Writer's Conference Anthology dated 1984 through
the Redwood Writing Project, Arcata, California: www.RedwoodWP.org
as *Blue Dandelion Puff.*)

EDEN

There are no fences in my backyard.
Emerald trees, bejeweled earth,
golden and opal light;
Warmth, softness and nutrients abound everywhere.
All are cared for even though they hold no job.
Air is fresh and doesn't burn.
There is joy in just breathing.
Silence is so natural, One can hear the Creator.
Every thing serves its own purpose
and supports the environment as well.
The only disruption is *civilization.*

ZOMBIE

Does anyone see the sunset anymore,
coloring the sky,
changing the lights and shadows?

People driving by
the nightly event;
High-Rises blocking the horizon;

Kept so busy,
that it all goes unseen,
and the grass grows for its own sake;

Ignoring the trees needing better air,
clean water,
neglecting the wildlife around;

Buzzing in our cells
is caffeine, sugars and preservatives
or in our ears with electronics;

Tuned out, disconnected,
what is real
has been recreated for us.

ANCIENT QUEEN

An atmospheric blanket
fills the sky
and insulates the ground;

A divine quiet,
the calm
before the warmth of day;

Not a soul is out;
The streets are vacant;
The Wild again owns the World;

Electricity in damp air;
Every limb, branch and living thing
stretching out to grow;

Like stealth itself, a Spirit Wanderer,
playing among the light spatterings and shadows,
full of energy fed by the living Earth;

Dancing among the boulevards and parking lots,
as if time and space did not exist.
Mo-'oh-peer's sheer gown gracefully blushes the city.

OF THE EARTH

The blood is warming;
The body comes alive;
The chest is full of anxiety.

Happiness abounds
in a semi-barren world.
It is time.

Within the week,
green starts are everywhere,
birds share their knowledge of the song.

It is Spring again.
Time for hope.
Time for awakening.

My blood runs like sap.
It is time to think about gathering stick;
Time for creating new Basket;

Born measuring time with a pulse,
hibernation is done.
It's time to grow with the natural environment.

SECRET PLACE

The wind filtering through the leaves,
a whisper
that life is more
than what you see;

White light peeks
through the canopy filter
gracing
 a lush green carpeted floor;

Around the corner,
gentle waves lap at the beach
and pull back the sand
to reveal gems.

A place where I can just be
...alone;
...myself;
...present in the moment.

[205]

PRIVILEGE

If people belong to the one spirit of Humanity,
and at their creation belong together,
born from another; giving birth to others...

then *individualization* grows abnormally
from circumstances
that seldom present themselves elsewhere in nature....

Beyond having basic needs met,
and thriving as the status quo,
is the next step counter-intuitive?

Possibly self-destructive?
...and how would that be measured,
but by the culture's own demise?

Like trees set aside on a sterile acre for preservation,
when the neighboring canopy is destroyed,
the remaining eventually dry and disease,

family bonds bleed by in-fighting,
torn by blind egocentrism;
Competition and jealousy now the norm;

With all Humanity's privilege, do we really know it all?
Has the previous generation truly been treasured
and privilege inherited...

or is destruction the natural course to our progress?

UNCEREMONEOUSLY

CEREMONY ROCK

Winter Sacred Place,
rising above the trees,
open to the sky,
towering over the Ocean;

You are the clown of the park
put up for display
with signs that mock
some mythical ceremony with no name;

Held out as a dog-and-pony show:
"Indians used to live here",
attracting people
who would exploit you;

Holes poked into your side
so that others can scale you
for recreation
and photo ops;

Garbage left behind,
you are objectified;
A no-name ceremony rock...
what does that really mean?

Dignity returning only during the winter months
when the First People return
and nature envelopes you again,
quiet and whole,

your true name honored.

[208]

*(Note - This Author supports educating Patrick's Point
Visitors about Yurok Ceremonial Rock.)*

INTERFERENCE

If you interfere with
the natural expression of things,
you remove the power of self determination
and then Nature will lean on you.

Are you strong enough to carry
the weight of the world
and
the
ramifications
that follow
...season after season;
Generations after generations,
and reflected back again
in the pool of life?

Hummingbird feeders,
the rock under the pond,
water bottles in the landfill,
damning the River,
telling a child his parent is not good.

Good,
bad,
or otherwise,
just
your
observation
changes
things.

SHADOW

What do you see?

The tree?

Its shadow?

Its spirit?

The surrounding environment?

The forest?

Or the thing that is missing?

...the thread of genocide?

[211]

RESEE THE WORLD

Indexes

[217]

YUROK - ENGLISH DICTIONARY

As Yurok language is an indigenous dialect, those words are listed first. This dictionary includes modern day common language as well to clarify concepts, however, words that can easily be found elsewhere such as professional and legal terms are not generally listed here. As the Yurok traditionally did not have a written language and there is a variety of spellings throughout time, words are therefore spelled as they sound, based upon the Yurok Language Project:"http://corpus.linguistics.berkeley.edu/~yurok/web/l exicon.html."

This Reference Dictionary is alphabetized, American-style for easy reference.

Bluecoat	Refers to soldiers who first came into the area. Their offspring were often called *Blue Children*.
Chah-chew	It is hard to do/it is difficult.
Chpuer-kok'	Gentleness.
Common knowledge	Words that are used often enough that most every (America-English) reader understands what is implied.
Cougar	Refers to American slang for a catty woman, typically a manipulator of less mature prey.
DSM	Diagnostic and Statistical Manual of Mental Disorders often used by professionals in order to identify client needs under billing codes.
DV	Jargon for domestic violence.

Good Road	Refers to the spiritually correct path in life.
Gram	Abbreviated for grandmother.
Hekw-sa'	Whale.
Indian	Refers to legal terminology assigned to North American First Peoples who were misnamed after the East Indies People which then became memorialized in the law and trickled down to common language. Specifically, *Indian* is used here to identify the local indigenous population.
Kay-get	Mountain lion.
Knaahl-koh	Placenta
Knok-see-mek'	I forget it, leave it (behind)
Minority	Refers to the American terminology allegedly describing underrepresented populations, but not necessarily representing the actual statistics.
Mo-'oh-peer	Fog.
Nerr-mer-yek'	I sing songs.

Old One	Refers to an elder, one of experience.
'Oo'	To exist.
'O-reen	To court a woman.
Paa'	No.
Pe-chan	Short, for a brief time.
Pkwe -ko-mey-ye-tek'	To bring out treasures carefully.
Pue-no-meehl	To cause illness in someone, create evil.
Quantum	Refers to the percentage of *Indian* Blood originally calculated by the Federal Government to be eligible for membership in a tribe; A genocidal tool.
Recipe	Refers to song, prayer, pattern, formula, mantra.
Rep-chem	Sugar (or honey).
Re-poh	Threshold/doorway.

Rez	*Indian* Slang for Reservation; Places the Federal Government assigned for *Indian* People to live.
Rote	Refers to rote or basic learning.
Sa-'a-wor'	Shadow, Shade.
Shape Shifter	There are different beliefs about what this is. Here it refers to the ability to alter consciousness which alters the way one exists and is viewed.
Soot-kok'	I am strong.
Sumeeg	Trinidad /Patrick's Point State Park area.
Teekw-tee-kwoh	To break into pieces.
Too'-mo-neehl	Be of value.
Trade Language	Refers to the legal case concerning the *Chinook Language*, wherein Treaty was made based upon common understanding of this *trade language* but was interpreted much differently by the parties involved.
Typo	Typographical error.

'Ue-ma-'ah	*Indian* Devil.
Visitor	Refers to Settlers, Colonists, Euro-Americans.
'Werrp'	Butterfly.
What's-His-Name	Refers to someone who isn't spoken about anymore due to improper deeds or death.
White	The term *"White"* is often used in this book in referring to European- Americans who hold that legal designation as described in the *Recommended Reading Section* of *Indexes,* Haney Lopez, I.L. (1996).
Wok-hlew	I give thanks.

Note - In some instances, a word is used in the singular when American language calls for the plural. This is usually done when a noun is referring to the spirit of a being which is infinite and whole as opposed to the common use or individual body of a being, which Americans may see as the totality of its life but it is actually only a part.

Note - Quotations or italicization are often used when quoting or citing popular rhetoric in this book, however, may not be the most appropriate word in actuality.

Note - Words intended as prayer are not interpreted here.

Note - Chapter number names are next to their numbers and are not included in the dictionary.

Note - Names that honor a living being or spirit are commonly capitalized.

Note - Yurok words are not used throughout this book so as to preserve the integrity of flow and easier understanding by non-speakers. When Yurok words are used, it is to be implied that more than the concept is being invoked by the reading. Not all Indian People speak their language as many languages were extinguished during the time of active Federal Indian Policy. World War II and Hollywood commemorative movies about Navajo Code Talkers helped Native languages gain support among non-Native populations. My Grandmother always said that words invoke great power, to take care of what was said as original words are closest to their true names and call to their essence. She rarely used her Original Language.

RECOMMENDED READINGS, WORKS CITED & CONSULTED:

Allport, G. W. (1979). *The nature of prejudice, 25th Anniversary Ed.* Perseus: Reading.

Banaji, M.R., Hardin, C. & Rothman, A.J. (1991). Implicit stereotyping in person judgment. *Journal of personality and social psychology,* vol. 65, no. 2, pp. 272-281.

Bargh, J.A., Chen, M. & Burrows, L. (1996). Automaticity of social behavior: Direct effects of trait construct and stereotype activation on action. *Journal of personality and social psychology,* vol. 71, no. 2, pp. 230-244.

Beck, P.V., Walters, A.L. & Francisco, N. (1977). *The sacred. Ways of knowledge. Sources of life.* Dine College Press: Tsaile.

Bell, M. (1962). *Karuk: the upriver people.* Naturegraph: Happy Camp.

Berg, I.K. & Kelly, S. (2000). *Building solutions in child protective services.* W.W. Norton & Co: New York.

Brizendine, L. (2006). *The female brain.* Morgan Road Books: New York.

Buckley, T. (2002). *Standing ground. Yurok Indian spirituality, 1950 - 1990.* University of California Press: Berkeley.

Canby, W.C. (1998). *American Indian law in a nutshell, 3d. Ed.* West Group: Minnesota.

[227]

Churchill, W. (1997). *A little matter of genocide. Holocaust and denial in the Americas 1492 to the Present.* City Lights: San Francisco.

Deloria, Jr., V. (1988). *Custer died for your sins. An Indian manifesto.* Macmillan: Norman.

Deloria, Jr., V. (1999). *Spirit and reason, The Vine Deloria, Jr. reader.* Fulcrum Publishing: Colorado.

Devine, P. G. (1989). Stereotypes and prejudice: their automatic and controlled components. *Journal of personality and social psychology,* vol. 56, no. 1, pp 5-18.

Dupris, J.C., Hill, K.S., & Rodgers, Jr. (2006). *The Si'lailo way. Indians, salmon and law on the Columbia River.* Carolina Academic Press: Durham.

Duran, E. & Duran, B. (1995). *Native American postcolonial psychology.* State University of New York Press: Albany.

Edinger, E.F. (1985). *Anatomy of the psyche - Alchemical symbolism in psychotherapy.* Open Court Publishing Company: Illinois.

Gaertner, S. L., Mann, J., Murrell, A. & Dovidio, J.F. (1989). Reducing intergroup bias: The benefits of recategorization. *Journal of personality and social psychology,* vol. 57, no. 2, pp 239-247.

Getches, D.H., Wilkinson, C.F. & Williams, R.A. (1998). *Cases and materials on federal Indian law, 4ᵗʰ Ed.* West Group: Minn.

Glick, P. & Fiske, S. (2001). An ambivalent alliance - hostile and benevolent sexism as complementary justifications for gender inequality. *American psychologist,* vol. 56, no. 2, pp. 109-118.

Haney Lopez, I.F. (1996). *White by law – The legal construction of race.* New York University Press: New York.

Harjo, J., Bird, G., Blanco, P. & Cuthand, B. (Eds). (1997). *Reinventing the enemy's language. Contemporary*

[228]

Native women's writings of North America. WW Norton & Co., Inc.: New York.

Hoxie, F. E. & Iverson, P. (Eds). (1998). *Indians in American history. An introduction. 2d edit.* Harlan Davidson: Wheeling.

Jones, M. (2002). *Social psychology of prejudice.* Prentice Hall: New Jersey.

Jung, C.G., Gerhard, A.& Hull, R.F.C. (1981). *The archetypes and the collective unconscious. Collected works of C.G. Jung, vol. 9, part 1.* Bolligen: Princeton.

Kroeber, A.L. (1976). *Yurok Myths.* University of California Press: London.

Levy, B. & Langer, E. (1994). Aging free from negative stereotypes: Successful memory in China and among the American deaf. *Journal of Personality and Social Psychology,* vol.66, no.6, pp 989-987.

Machiavelli, N. (1952). *The Prince* (L. Ricci, Trans). Oxford University Press: New York.

Margolin, M. (Ed.). (1981). *The way we lived. California Indian stories, songs & reminiscences.* Heyday books: Berkley

Mehl-Madrona, L. (M.D.) (1997) *Coyote medicine. Lessons from Native American healing.* Fireside: New York.

Meier, J.S. (2009). *Parental alienation syndrome and parental alienation: research reviews. VAWNet:*Harrisburg. www.vawnet.org

Miller, J.G. (1998) *Last one over the wall: The Massachusetts experiment in closing reform schools (2Ed).* Ohio State University Press: Columbus.

Modesto, R. & Mount, G. (1980). *Not for innocent ears. Spiritual traditions of a Desert Cahuilla medicine woman.* Sweetlight: Arcata.

Ohlheiser, K.L. (2010). *The love of agates.* Blurb, Inc.: San Francisco. www.blurb.com

[229]

Prucha, F.P. (Ed.) (2000). *Documents of United States Indian policy, 3rd Ed.* University of Nebraska Press: Lincoln.

Raphael, R. & House, F. (2007). *Two peoples, one place - Humboldt history, Vol. 1.* Humboldt County Historical Society: California.

Richardson, P. (2006). *A kidnapped mind. A mother's heartbreaking story of parental alienation syndrome.* Dundurn: Toronto.

Ritzer, G. (2001). The McDonaldization of society. In J.M. Henslin (Ed.), *Down to earth sociology, 11th Ed. (*pp 459-471). Free Press: New York.

Roberts, D. (1997). *Killing the Black body. Race, reproduction, and the meaning of liberty.* Random House: New York.

Ruggiero, V.R. (2001), *The art of thinking. A guide to critical and creative thought. 6th Ed.* Addison Wesley Longman, Inc.: New York.

Scales, T.L. & Streeter, C. L. Editors (2004). *Rural social work. Building and sustaining community assets.* Thomson Brooks/Cole: Belmont.

Spott, R. & Kroeber, A.L. (1997). *Yurok narratives.* University of California Press: Berkeley.

Stannard, D. E. (1992). *The conquest of the new world. American holocaust.* Oxford University Press: New York.

Steele, C. (1997). A threat in the air. How stereotypes shape intellectual identity and performance. *American psychologist*, vol. 52, no. 6, pp 613-629.

Suppes, M. & Wells, C. (2003). *The social work experience. An introduction to social work and social welfare (4th Ed.).* McGraw-Hill: New York.

The Bible. King James Version.

The gene and the genome edition. (October 19, 2001). *TLS Newspaper.*

Thompson, L. (1991) *To the American Indian. Reminiscences of a Yurok woman.* HeyDay: Berkeley.

Tzu, L. (1961). *Tao Teh Ching.* St. John's University Press: New York.

Weaver, H.N. (2005) *Explorations in cultural competence. Journeys to the four directions.* Thomson Brooks/Cole: Belmont.

Note - Citations are included on the page they reference and may not be included in the *Recommended Readings Index.*

PHOTO CREDITS
(Photographer: Katie L. Ohlheiser)

[233]

COVER: Village House at
                                    Sumeeg, more
                                    commonly referred to
                                    as Patrick's Point State
                                    Park, Trinidad, CA.

COPYRIGHT PAGE: Sumeeg, CA

DISCLAIMER PAGE: Sumeeg Village Sweat
                                    Lodge, Trinidad, CA.

DEDICATION: Pacific Ocean at
                                    Sumeeg, Agate Beach,
                                    Trinidad, CA.

FOREWORD: Edge of the Continent,
                                    Northern California.

CHAPTER TITLE/END PAGES: Various Victorian
                                    doors from Sacramento
                                    and Eureka, CA.

'Oo' PHOTOS:

TREATY: Korbel, CA, Lioness
                                    Club of 1966 marked
                                    this Redwood as the
                                    treaty tree between the
                                    "Mountain and Coastal
                                    Indians".

RUNAWAY: Graffiti,
                                    Sumeeg, CA

Pkwe-ko-mey-ye-tek' PHOTOS:

VEIN:	Sumeeg, CA
INTERNAL CLOCK:	Sumeeg, CA
DANDELION:	Sumeeg, CA
EDEN:	Sumeeg, CA
ZOMBIE:	Eureka, CA
ANCIENT QUEEN:	Loleta, CA
OF THE EARTH:	Sumeeg, CA
SECRET PLACE:	Sumeeg, CA
UNCEREMONEOUSLY:	Sumeeg, CA
CEREMONY ROCK:	Sumeeg, CA
SHADOW	Sumeeg, CA
RESEE THE WORLD	Church window, Sacramento, CA
INDEXES:	Victorian window from Eureka, CA
YUROK-ENGLISH DICTIONARY:	Sumeeg Village Houses
RECOMMENDED READINGS:	Victorian window from Eureka, CA

[235]

PHOTO CREDITS: Sumeeg, CA

AUTHOR'S PAGE: Author at time of
                       second publishing,
                       2011, Humboldt State
                       University, Arcata, CA

LAST PAGE: Sumeeg Village House
                       Threshold looking out
                       into Patrick's Point
                       State Park, Trinidad,
                       CA. The belief of
                       going out of the door is
                       that One is reborn each
                       day.

ABOUT THE AUTHOR:

Katie L. Ohlheiser lives in Humboldt County, California. While her ancestors come from various backgrounds, her legal status is as a Northwest California Native, the seventh generation from contact. Katie comes to know her culture and the direct effects of genocide from her maternal linage as these American *Indian* mothers had the role of raising the children and keeping the culture alive during the active history of Federal Indian Policy. Her People retain traditional knowledge and ancient truths handed down since time immemorial.

Katie found refuge and hope through the intervention of the California Indian Education Program, eventually becoming the first in her immediate family to graduate from a university (with honors). Katie graduated from Humboldt State University in 2006 with the inaugural Masters of Social Work class; 2004 with a Bachelor's Degree in Native American Studies and a minor in psychology.

Katie has been active with First Nations populations as a possibility worker/social worker, lecturer and cultural expert witness. Katie is passionate about removing racism, objectification and discrimination from the American language and institutions, of which this book is among her efforts.

[239]

There is no such thing as an End.

Only rebirth and new possibilities.

wok-hlew wok-hlew wok-hlew